Kitchen Witchcraft:
The Element of Fire

Kitchen Witchcraft: The Element of Fire

Rachel Patterson

MOON
BOOKS

Winchester, UK
Washington, USA

JOHN HUNT PUBLISHING

First published by Moon Books, 2022
Moon Books is an imprint of John Hunt Publishing Ltd., No. 3 East Street, Alresford
Hampshire SO24 9EE, UK
office@jhpbooks.net
www.johnhuntpublishing.com
www.moon-books.net

For distributor details and how to order please visit the 'Ordering' section on our website.

Text copyright: Rachel Patterson 2021

ISBN: 978 1 78904 721 9
978 1 78904 722 6 (ebook)
Library of Congress Control Number: 2021935828

A CIP catalogue record for this book is available from the British Library.

Design: Matthew Greenfield

UK: Printed and bound by CPI Group (UK) Ltd, Croydon, CR0 4YY
Printed in North America by CPI GPS partners

We operate a distinctive and ethical publishing philosophy in
all areas of our business, from our global network of authors to
production and worldwide distribution.

Contents

The fifth book in the Kitchen Witchcraft series along with *Spells & Charms,*
Garden Magic, Crystal Magic and *The Element of Earth.*

This book will focus on the element of Fire; what it is, the correspondences, how to work with it, fire elementals, meditations, rituals and basically everything fire related.

Let's light the fire...

Who am I?

I am a Pagan Witch, working wife and mother who has also been lucky enough to write and have published a fair number of books on the Craft. I love to learn, I love to study and have done so from books, online resources, schools and wonderful mentors over the past thirty years or so and continue to learn every day but have learnt the most from getting outside and doing it. I am High Priestess of the Kitchen Witch Coven and an Elder at the online Kitchen Witch School.

I like to laugh, bake and eat cake...

www.rachelpatterson.co.uk
facebook.com/rachelpattersonbooks

www.kitchenwitchhearth.net
facebook.com/kitchenwitchuk
Email: HQ@kitchenwitchhearth.net

I also have regular blogs on:

Patheos Pagan
www.patheos.com/blogs/beneaththemoon

Witches & Pagans
www.witchesandpagans.com/pagan-paths-blogs/hedge-witch.
html

My craft is a combination of old religion Witchcraft, Kitchen Witchery,
Hedge Witchery and folk magic. My heart is that of a Kitchen Witch.

MY BOOKS

Kitchen Witchcraft Series
Spells & Charms
Garden Magic
Crystal Magic
The Element of Earth

Pagan Portals
Kitchen Witchcraft
Hoodoo Folk Magic
Moon Magic
Meditation
The Cailleach
Animal Magic
Sun Magic
Triple Goddess

Other Moon Books
The Art of Ritual
Beneath the Moon
Witchcraft ... into the Wilds
Grimoire of a Kitchen Witch
A Kitchen Witch's World of Magical Foods
A Kitchen Witch's World of Magical Plants & Herbs
Arc of the Goddess (co–written with Tracey Roberts)
Moon Books Gods & Goddesses Colouring Book (Patterson family)
Practically Pagan: An Alternative Guide to Cooking

Llewellyn
Curative Magic

Fire within me
Flames around me
Passion beyond me
Energy fills me

The Basics

The elements are the original foundation of which all other things are made, by unification or transformation. The ancients divided the world into four basic elements which we know as Earth, Fire, Air, and Water. These four elements are vital to our survival for without any one of them we could not exist. The four elements, five if you count ether/spirit, make up the base foundation of magic. We use them in ritual, energy work, healing and spell work.

We are all probably drawn more to one element than the others. They each have their own unique characteristics and properties that we can tap in to. They can be used individually or mix 'n match to add power. I do think it helps to have a balance of them all.

Fire is a little different from the other three elements as it cannot be physically touched without causing injury. It naturally exists in our sun but must be created here on earth and so it can be said that it doesn't have a natural home. We need the element of fire to grow and cook our food and to keep us warm in winter.

Fire is the element of action, passion, transformation and of change. Fire rules all forms of magic, because magic is the process of change, but fire is destructive and will consume and destroy before change can happen. Passion, the sacred fire of sex, the spark of divinity which shines within all living things are associated with the element of fire. This element also rules transformation, will, fear, anger, power, jealousy, purification, energy, strength, power, achievement, life, and ecstatic dance. Fire also rules physical things and places such as blood, sap, deserts, volcanoes, the sun and fires of all varieties, from a simple candle flame to an eruption or explosion.

The place of fire in most witchcraft traditions is in the south of the ritual circle, it is associated with midday and the height

1

of summer. You will often find a candle on an altar to represent the element of fire. Early man would probably have only encountered fire when something was struck by lightning and so it would be fair to say that they would have thought it was something magical, sent to them from the heavens. We now use it as a spiritual focus whether that is as a hearth fire or ritual flame.

Here are a few of my own fire correspondences:

Gender – Masculine
Animals – Dragon, lion, bee, phoenix, coyote, fox, lizard, snake, cricket, praying mantis, shark, squirrel, porcupine, badger, coyote, fox, cat, bear, rabbit, hawk, horse
Colour – Black, orange, red, white, yellow
Direction – South
Divination – Candle and fire scrying
Energy – Projective
Time – Noon
Magic – Candle, burning, manifesting, burn petitions, scrying, burning herbs, fire, light, heat
Magical Tool – Athame, sometimes the wand
Musical Instrument – Guitar, string instruments
Symbols – Flames, lava
Places – Deserts, volcanoes, gyms, ovens, fireplaces, hot springs, bedrooms, gym, locker room, sauna, athletic field
Spell work/Rituals/Positive Qualities – Courage, change, energy, protection, strength, passion, personal power, ingenuity, manifesting, will power, bravery, beginnings, drive, action, death and rebirth, movement, ideas, change, sensuality, purification, breaking bad habits, authority, banishing, transformation, negativity, sex, authority, speed, creativity, destruction, cleansing, sexuality, force, motion, anger, desire, work, freedom
Negatives: Anger, jealousy, stubbornness, greed, arrogance,

resentment, possessiveness, cruelty, violence
Season – Summer
Spirits – Salamanders
Zodiac – Aries, Leo and Sagittarius
Tarot – The suit of Wands
Pentagram position – Lower right
Archangel – Michael

PLEASE... (I know I don't really need to say this) if you are in the woods or forest area check that you are allowed to start a fire (a lot of places don't give permission for obvious reasons). If you are given the go ahead make sure you take the proper precautions and don't let it get out of hand. A fire in the woods or grassy fields can cause a huge amount of damage not only to the land and plants but also to the animals that live there.

Scrying with flames is great fun, you don't need to use a bonfire/campfire/fireplace you can just use a candle, but you get brilliant images with a full 'set' of flames. Be mindful that fire is a fickle thing and it does like to play games with your mind though.

You don't need anything special to scry with flames other than...flames...once the fire is going nicely sit back and relax, ground yourself and then gaze into the flames. Watch for any symbols that you might see not just in the flames but also in the glowing embers and the smoke.

Also, listen careful because sometimes the fire may speak to you. You might get very clear images or even hear words but equally you may just get flashes of images, symbols or sounds that you will need to translate. If you have some herbs to hand you can throw them onto the fire to get some interesting shapes and smoke, try using the woodier herbs.

If you have a back garden you can use a fire pit or chimenea very successfully for fire magic. However, if your space is limited you can work with a cast iron cauldron or a fire proof dish.

Simple workings can be done by using small slips of paper. If you want to get rid of a bad habit then write it down on a piece of paper and throw that into the fire. You might also like to create a chant to go with it or add in some corresponding herbs. Similarly, if you are having a run of bad luck you can write that down on the paper and burn it. Gossip can be stopped by writing the rumours on paper and throwing it into the flames.

Exercise
Light a fire or a candle and just spend some time watching the flame/s. Look at the colours, feel the heat and experience the energy.

The Elemental You

Most of us will find that we are aligned more with one element than another. This may be affected by the zodiac sign we were born under. It may also be because of the work we do or the life we lead. Every mundane task carries a correspondence to one of the elements. The challenge is to create balance in ourselves between all four elements. You might like to make a list to see which element you are heavy in and which ones you may need to work a little more with to bring about balance. Let's look at the everyday element of fire related tasks:

- Cooking
- Creativity – art, baking, crafting, designing
- De-cluttering
- Music – listening, playing an instrument
- Dancing – professional or just good ole 'dad dancing'
- Driving a vehicle
- Sun bathing
- Lighting a fire
- Turning on the heating
- Turning on a light switch

- Plugging in an electrical device (phone charger, hair dryer etc)
- Workout/physical exercise
- Working at your computer
- Using your mobile phone

Exercise

Make a list of all your daily chores and activities. Separate them into elements. Which element has the longest list? Which has the shortest? What could you do to help balance your elements out?

Fire Energy

As we work with the positive and negative, sun and moon, masculine and feminine, energy too has opposites. Those of receptive and projective. The flow of energy for fire is projective. Projective energy is described as being masculine, it is heat, the summer, activity, outward, physical and brings light. Projective energy is good for strength, healing, protection, vitality, courage, power, determination, will power, self-confidence, luck and success.

We can connect with the element of fire in many ways. The obvious ones are practical such as lighting a fire or candles. But there are also magical ways to connect as well (many are suggested within this book), such as working with candle magic and raising energy. There are mundane chores that also connect us to the element of fire, such as cooking or creating in your kitchen.

Just a reminder…when you work with energy, don't draw it from within yourself. That can be extremely draining and cause you to become very tired or even poorly. Use your body as a channel for the energy. Mother Earth is very happy to lend you the energy you need, all you must do is draw it from her and channel it to where you want it to go.

Fire Magic

Several types of magic lend themselves to working with the fire element.

Candle magic – probably one of the most used types of magic. It can be as simple as lighting a birthday cake candle. White candles are useful as they cover all intents. Colour magic comes into play with candles, with each colour representing a different intent. For instance, a red candle will often be used for passion and a yellow one for happiness. There are traditional colours associated with each intent, but I encourage you to trust your own intuition. Candles can be dressed in magical essential oil blends and then rolled in ground herbs and spices, each adding a layer of power and magic to the candle spell. Crystals can also be placed around the base of a candle to add power when working the spell. Visualisation is called for, as with most spell work. Light your candle and visualise your desires and goals.

Burning – one of my favourites ways to work magic is to burn stuff. This can be a simple case of adding a pinch of herbs into a bonfire or writing my desire on a sage leaf and setting light to it from a candle flame (dropping it into a fire proof dish to burn). Slips of paper or lists can be written on, folded and set alight to burn. Herbs, twigs and leaves can be thrown ceremonially onto fires. A Yule log is always burnt on an open fire. You can use a candle flame and a fire proof dish. Cast iron cauldrons are useful for having very small fires in. Fire pits and chimineas are very good for small contained fires and of course bonfires are King!

Despacho – this idea is based on a shamanic tradition from Peru which has some beautiful rituals involved. I would like to share my witchy version with you. The idea is that the despacho is an offering bundle used for all sorts of intentions. Think of it as a spell parcel. The contents are symbolic to the intent and the people involved. The contents need to be biodegradable and able to burn without releasing any nasties into the air. Go with things such as herbs, spices, grains, sugars, leaves, twigs, seeds, flowers, incense, paper, feathers, dried pulses, salt, string/twine and bark. You will need a large sheet of paper to wrap it all up in and some string.

You can make your despacho part of a ritual ceremony by casting a circle, calling the quarters and all the bells and whistles a ritual brings. Or you can just sit quietly in your own sacred space and create the despacho, just giving a few words of prayer or blessing.

Lay the sheet of paper out and start adding your contents. Say a few words and charge each piece and place it onto the paper. Trust your intuition about where and how each item should be placed on the paper. Once you feel all the items have been placed that are needed, carefully fold the paper so that it wraps all the contents securely. Tie it with string or twine.

Say a few last words to secure the spell, then place the despacho into a fire, a bonfire or fire pit would be perfect. Stay with the parcel as it burns and preferably until the flames have died down to embers. Allow the fire to burn out naturally. Once the ashes are cold, bury them in the earth.

Scrying – flames from the fire or candle flame and smoke can all be used for divination.

Sun magic – this is of course a whole book's worth of subject on its own (and yes, I may just have a book already published on the subject – Pagan Portals Sun Magic.). A lot of focus is placed on working moon magic with her various phases, but the sun has phases too. The bonus is that the sun has all of its phases within one day (rather than waiting for a whole month with the moon). You can work magic with the sun phases at different times of the day. Or just work with a sun god or the energy of the sun as a whole to give your spell work a big boost of magic. The energy of the sun works particularly well with the element of fire and any associated spells.

Ash– whenever I have a ritual fire, whether it is for a sabbat, sun or moon phase, I like to save the ash from the fire. I place scoopfuls of the cold ash in jars and label with the sabbat, sun or moon phase. Then I have ash to add to any further spell work. It can also be used to draw sigils or symbols on surfaces. It can be added to spell pouches, witch bottles or roll candles in the ash for candle magic. You could also try divination with ashes from a fire too.

Charcoal – you are probably all familiar with the charcoal discs we use to light and then sprinkle loose incense on. They can be a nightmare to light when you are standing in the middle of a field! I find at home the best way to light them is grab a charcoal disc between metal tongs and hold it over a naked flame, I do this on my gas burner. Once the charcoal is sparkling and spitting it is lit, leave it for a minute or two to calm down then add your incense.

Cleansing with smoke – Perhaps associated with the element of air, but I think it also aligns with fire. The burning of herbs to create smoke for psychic and spiritual cleansing is found in many religions across many cultures. The term smudging is often used, this now seems to refer to the Native American practice of using herb bundles to cleanse the energy field of a person, object or room. However, my research discovered that the word 'smudge' comes from the old English word 'smogen'. (You will find the definition in several dictionaries such as Merriam Webster and Collins). The word comes from late middle English in the 1400s. Smogen means to smear, blur, obscure, to smother with smoke, to use dense smoke to protect an area from insects. In modern

English the word smudge also means to smut or dirt. It has been in use since the 15th Century and is of Germanic origin. The idea behind smudging with smoke is that the smoke attaches itself to the negative energy and as it disperses it takes the negative energy with it. I like to smudge on a regular basis, my home, my altars and myself. Whilst the Native Americans traditionally use white sage, sweetgrass or cedar, I like to use something that grows more locally to me. Being in England, white sage is not native to my location. However, I have plenty of green garden sage, lavender and rosemary in my garden that I like to create my smudge bundles from. Ancient Vikings would have used Mugwort as that grew wild.

Please don't import dried herbs from across the globe. Use an herb or plant that grows locally to you. A local herb will have more personal energy but will also be far more eco-friendly without all the transportation damage. You can make your own bundle by cutting stems of the plants, tying them together with wool or twine and leaving them to dry. Once dried, it is ready to use.

Light one end of the bundle and then blow out the flame so it is just smouldering, it is wise to hold the bundle over a bowl to catch anything bits that may fall off, it saves burning holes in the carpet. You can guide the smoke over yourself by using a feather or your hands (whichever you prefer). Bring the smoke up over your head, down your shoulders and your arms. Around your torso and your back, down your left and your feet, not forgetting to do the soles to ensure that you walk on the right path. Visualise the smoke lifting away all the negative energies, thoughts and emotions that have attached themselves to you. When you are cleansing your house make sure the smoke gets into all the corners, around the windows and doors, and if you want to be really thorough you can waft it in all the cupboards and drawers too.

Whether you are cleansing yourself or your home this needs

there needs to be a structure to this. It becomes a bit of a ritual. Just wafting smoke around haphazardly won't do. You need your will and intent behind it and some effort. Decide whether you want to go around the room clockwise or anti clockwise. Really think about your actions and the way you waft the smoke. It helps to have a chant to go with it. You can say what you feel, but make sure you have real intent behind it. Or write out a proper chant to use each time. Follow a pattern and make it a bit ceremonial. The end result will be much better if you have made some effort with it.

When you have finished make sure your herb bundle is extinguished using a bowl of sand or earth. Make sure the herb stick is completely out before leaving it. Of course, if you are like me then you will find the herb bundle a bit awkward to use sometimes and that's when you can use loose herbs on a charcoal block or for even more convenience a shop bought incense stick will do the job just as well. It is your intention that is important. If you can't stand the smoke, then try with an oil burner or scented candles. You can also pop loose incense onto an oil burner, allowing the candle to just warm the mix without the smoke.

Cord Cutting – This type of magic is used to help you separate and/or distance yourself from someone that is no longer good for you. It doesn't need to be a person it can also help remove you from situations, issues and places. All cord cutting magic involves a cord of some kind obviously, but it can be a physical cord or visualised. I include this in with the element of fire because it involves transformation and changes but can also include burning the cord or petition with flame in the ritual.

Lanterns/torches – Before the advent of electricity a lot of homes would use oil lamps, these can be used effectively in magic. Herbs, roots and a drop or two of essential oil can be added to the reservoir of the lamp. You can also drop in small crystals or minerals too. Personalise the lamp to the intent of the spell you wish to work. I would suggest that when adding essential oils to the reservoir, you keep to natural oils, nothing that will cause an explosion or toxic gases!

Petition or name papers can then be added, prepared in the usual manner and pinned to the wick of the oil lamp. You don't even need to use a readymade oil lamp, they can easily be made from coffee tins, hurricane lamps or even natural items such as a coconut shell.

Incense – although this is often representative of the element of air, I think it also crosses over to fire as well. Incense comes in several forms; you can create your own loose incense blends to burn on charcoal discs. Incense cones and sticks are very easy to get hold of and work extremely well.

If you want to create your own loose incense, start with a base, a resin is good such as frankincense or copal. Adding a wood of some sort helps your incense to burn longer too, or if you are using home grown dried herbs the woody stems of herbs can be added in. Then the choice is up to you, whether you go for the scent you like or for the intent. Incense can be made for prosperity, love, success etc but you can also make incense to correspond with the moon phase, a sabbat, a particular ritual or to honour a specific deity.

I also like to add a few drops of essential oil to my incense mix once I have finished it, just to give it an extra boost of scent and power.

Remember as well that incense put together for magical purpose may not always smell particularly pleasant, it is the energies of the herbs that are important. I would also suggest keeping it simple, too many ingredients and it gets complicated. Less is more as they say. Don't forget that loose incense burnt on charcoal makes quite a bit of smoke.

Curses, hexes and bindings– Knowledge is power. If you know about curses and hexes then you are fore-warned and fore-armed. If you choose to hex or curse then that of course is your right to do so, just be mindful of the backlash…

I am also not going to get on a soap box and spout off about morals, taking the high ground, karma etc – that choice is yours to make, and yours alone. My personal thoughts are: If you get cross or upset about something or with someone; stop and think. Don't just blindly work a spell to curse or hex someone in the heat of anger. Let the hurt die down first, and then decide what course of action to take.

Sometimes there are situations that warrant action or reaction and sometimes it is not easy to decide what course to follow. A good rule of thumb to follow is if you would not do it in reality then don't do it with magic. Make sure that what you do, whatever kind of defensive action you take is equivalent to the action that was taken against you. Think about your plan of action, if you feel uncomfortable in any way then don't do it, go back to the drawing board and come up with Plan B, C or D (and all the rest of the letters in the alphabet if need be).

Curses and hexes are not for the faint hearted and if you decide that is the path you want to go down, I urge you to not take them lightly and never chuck them about willy nilly – take responsibility for your actions. You also need to be very, very sure that the person you are sending a curse or hex to is the person responsible…

Okay, so let's look at what hexes and curses are: Just as there are hundreds and thousands of love and prosperity spells there are probably just as many hexes. Some of them involve long complicated rituals, some require all sorts of ingredients and others are just gestures with a hand or a word.

So, what is the difference between a hex and a curse? Well, I am not sure there is much of a difference to be honest, just different names from diverse cultures. However, the consensus seems to be that a hex is a spell or bewitchment, traditionally they could be good or bad and a Witch could be paid to provide one. A curse is a malevolent spell that is cast with the purpose of inflicting harm upon another; curses can be spoken or written. Objects can also be cursed with bad luck, misfortune, ill health and even death.

Essentially, it's the wilful direction of negative energy towards someone with the intent to harm. Usually hexes and curses take some time to develop, building up slowly. However, if you are well shielded and protected you are very unlikely to become the victim of a hex yourself and I think it happens a lot less frequently than people believe.

Binding – I would also like to look at binding; this is a form of spell that binds a person or situation so that they/it can no longer harm you. I have found this form of working particularly successful, if you are pure in your intent, it doesn't harm the person or cause them any discomfort it just stops them from hurting or harassing you. Bear in mind this spell does take away the free will of the person you are binding, so use with caution.

A binding spell can be very simple – you use an object that represents the person causing you harm – it can be a poppet; it could be a photograph or it might just be a potato that you have identified as the person. It can then be bound, with string, ribbon or even sticky tape. As you bind the object visualise binding the harmful energies of that person and speak your wishes, that the person can no longer harm you or harass you. Bury or burn the spell.

Banishing – On to banishing, now I have had a lot of experience with this and not all of it has been good. I thought it sounded like a lovely idea to 'banish negative energy' from my life. What I didn't expect was the huge circle that this type of banishing covers. It does not just get rid of bad luck it covers all sorts of things...including people. To banish all negative energy from your life is not always a good thing. We all need balance in life, for instance think about batteries they need positive and negative to work, and if you took away the negative, they would have no power.

Much better to ask that "any negative energy that serves me no good be released", it's safer believe me. Note I used the word 'release' rather than 'banish', I have found it is safer. But please be prepared for unexpected results...

A very simple banishing spell is to use some slips of paper and a cauldron. Write what you want to banish on the slips of paper, light the corner of each slip on a candle and drop it into the cauldron, visualising the feeling/emotion/bad habit/ whatever disappearing. Send the ashes out into the wind or into running water (or even down the toilet).

PLEASE remember that whatever you banish leaves a hole, that hole must be purposely filled with positive energy otherwise it will just be replaced with that which is similar to what you wanted to get rid of in the first place. I find it wise to add onto the end of a banishing something like "and fill the void with love and blessings". And remember that banishing often take some time to work too.

Sex Magic – Perhaps not something that everyone wants to work with, but it does align with the energy of the element of fire. It is passion, energy and a huge amount of personal power. I feel the need to state here; only work with sex magic if you feel it is right for you and if you are comfortable with it. I would only recommend working sex magic as a couple if you BOTH feel comfortable with it. Never do anything that doesn't feel right for you. Sex magic brings about manifesting, releasing and transformation.

The obvious build-up of energy that sex brings and then the release in orgasm works in perfect harmony with spell work.

Whether on your own or with a partner the energy is undeniable. If you are working with a partner then you will need to agree on an intent so that you can direct the energy to the same purpose. Sex can be total raw power but also think about the spiritual side of it. When you involve the spirituality as well it can become a very powerful and magical experience. The premise of this is the same as it would be with any ritual that includes a spell. You prepare, you might even cast a full circle, you raise the power, you visualise your intent/goal and then you release the energy. Sex magic is a huge subject and one that covers many different aspects.

Hearth Magic – As a Kitchen Witch this area is one of my favourites to work with. This is all about cooking, baking and brewing. When you use your oven, you are using the magic of fire. When you make bread, cookies or cake or anything that involves bringing ingredients together you are being creative which is associated with the element of fire. There is a whole magical area that covers food (that is another book...A Kitchen Witch's World of Magical Food). It is a huge subject and if it interests you, I wholeheartedly encourage you to explore. Magical sigils can be put into bread, cakes and cookies. Ingredients can be charged with intent as you add them to recipes. Every food has a magical correspondence and this can be used in your recipes. The actions you make when creating food all have symbolism. Stirring clockwise brings in positive energy, anti clockwise releases negative energy. The kitchen is the heart of the home and everything you do in there is creative and filled with fire energy. This doesn't just cover food; your kitchen is probably the place that you create your lotions and potions in as well.

Horseshoes – You may be lucky enough to find a horseshoe when you are out and about on your travels and I think they, along with blacksmiths, are very magical. Definitely a strong connection with the element of fire from both the metal and the forge within which they were made.

There is a very big connection between horseshoes and the Fairy folk, horse shoes being made of iron and the fair folk having a great aversion to the stuff. The Fairy were blamed for all sorts of mishaps within the house such as things going missing, milk going sour and chickens not laying and to be honest they probably were responsible for a great number of those things. The belief was spread that Fairies did not like iron and so apparently people started hanging iron horseshoes on their front doors as protection. The horseshoe not only had the protective quality of being iron but it is also shaped like the moon which also had power.

There are two schools of thought; one is that the horseshoe should be hung points upwards to stop the good luck from falling out and the second believe that the points should be downwards so that the luck pours out over those people walking through the doorway.

Another branch of folklore believed that the horseshoe was a symbol of the moon goddess and hanging the horseshoe over your door brought blessings and protection from the goddess. There is also the suggestion that a horseshoe hung points downwards represented the feminine energy of the Irish goddess Sheela na Gig or the Christian Virgin Mary the inference being that the horseshoe was shaped like a yoni...obviously, they had a lot of time on their hands to think about things...

The horseshoe was also hung over doorways points downwards so that no witch would be able to pass under it and enter the house.

In some cultures, the horseshoe is hung in the house and touched to bring luck and in Mexico there is a tradition of wrapping the horseshoe in coloured thread and decorating with holy prints and a prayer.

The horseshoe shape as a symbol has been adopted for luck

and used in all manner of items such as jewellery to bring luck to gamblers particularly. Also, because it is shaped somewhat like a magnet so it can be used to 'draw' money to you in magical workings.

There are many stories all along the same theme about the blacksmith and the devil. Such as, the devil appearing inside a smithy one day and demanding that the blacksmith fit him with his own iron shoes. The blacksmith realising that it was the devil made a shoe and nailed it to the devil's hoof whilst it was still burning hot. The devil was in such pain that he ripped off the shoe and swore never to go back to a smithy again. Horseshoes were therefore hung over the entrance of a house to ward against the devil and any evil spirits.

The horseshoe is traditionally made from iron which was the strongest known metal to our ancestors and it was also attached to the horse using seven nails, seven was thought to be a lucky number. Horses, of course, have their own power and strength and when walking on cobblestones the metal of the horse shoe could have thrown off sparks which would have added to the magic. And of course, iron itself would have been magical because it was taken from the earth and could withstand fire and cold so it would have been very highly regarded.

Iron is also associated with male sexual energy and carries a heap load of potent sex magic with it, think of the power and virility of a stallion...

Healing horseshoe: To relieve a headache hold a horseshoe against your forehead, visualise the pain leaving you and transferring into the horseshoe.

Whatever the reasons for the belief, a horseshoe can be turned into a very effective protective or lucky charm and the symbol can be used in all kinds of magical workings.

Time

Another association for the elements is the time of day. Fire links with noon, right slap bang in the middle of the day when the sun is at its highest point in the sky. If you want to add a fiery boost of power to your spell working then time your magic to happen at high noon, twelve o'clock.

Exercise
Work spells at different times and record the results, does it make a difference?

Symbols

Probably the most recognised symbols for the elements are the triangles. Fire is represented by an upward pointing triangle. The upward triangle represents the male form and symbolises action and movement. If you want to represent fire on your altar, in ritual or for spell work there are several items you can use.

A candle is perhaps one of the most obvious
Matches or a lighter
Chillies or black pepper
Ash – a little dish filled with fire ash
Crystals – lots of crystals are associated with the element of fire (see crystal reference in this book)
Charcoal disc – makes sense to me that this could represent fire
Lantern – an oil lantern or one that holds a candle

Lamp – could be just a simple table lamp or a fancy one

Horseshoe or iron nails – iron brings the element of fire in full force

Exercise

Take a look at your altar, what items do you have placed on it and why are they there? What elements do you have represented?

The Athame/Dagger

There was a little indecision about what magical tool to include here. The athame or dagger is often given as the fire element magical tool. However, if you work with tarot then in most decks Wands are associated with fire (the swords are air). To solve this dilemma, I put a poll on the Kitchen Witch Coven Facebook group, it was overwhelming in the response. The athame is the magical tool of choice when it comes to associations with the element of fire. So that is the magical tool I shall go with (which was actually my personal choice in the beginning anyway). I guess it also depends on what your use your athame for. If you are using it to control energy, cut doorways, cast circles and generally transform space, then for me it associated with fire.

The athame or dagger if you prefer, is a ceremonial knife. Traditionally it is often a black handle with a double knife edge. Although the edge is not usually sharp enough for it to be used practically. Which is perhaps wise, you don't want to be waving around a very sharp blade when in the middle of a ritual circle. It is used for casting ritual circles, invoking and banishing. There are some beautiful athames on the market but you could use a plain knife, a vegetable knife or even a vegetable peeler would work well. If you find one with a wooden handle you could carve symbols into it or paint them on to personalise it. The athame is a representation of the God, of masculine energy.

The term 'athame' seems to have arrived in the late 1940's from our good old friend Gerald Gardner. His fiction book 'High

Magic's Aid' featured the use of a ritual knife that he called an 'athame'. Why did he come up with that name? Well, I guess we won't ever know for sure but there are some suggestions that it was a variation on several words. The Key of Solomon (a grimoire from the 14th/15th Century) features the words artave, arthane and arthame in the French translations of the book. The Latin word 'artavus' describes a specific type of knife. A couple of books from the late 1920's also feature similar words. Arthana is used in the book 'The Mysteries and Secrets of Magic' by C J S Thompson, it describes a magical tool. And Grillot de Givry mentions an arthame in his book 'Witchcraft, Magic and Alchemy'. There is also an old French word 'attame' that translates as 'to cut or piece'.

Even though the name athame is perhaps quite recent, the use of knives in ritual is ancient. The knife as a useful tool has been used by man for an extremely long time. Perhaps one of the first tools he ever made to help cut, hunt and carve. There is even archaeological evidence that ancient man created knives for ceremonial or religious purpose as well as useful tools.

Circa 4500 BCE, the good ole ancient Egyptians loved ceremonial knives for religious purpose and of course…sacrificial ones too. These ceremonial knives were often intricately carved with animals and symbols.

British Bronze Age man (2500 to 800 BCE) often buried their dead with a dagger, whether to help them in the afterlife or for some other unknown purpose, who knows? A 13th Century book, 'Grimoire of Honorius' includes using a knife as a ritual tool, just as the 14th/15th Century book the 'Key of Solomon' does. These books talk about casting circles and invoking the directions. Both the 'Key of Solomon' and some Jewish Grimoires from the 16th Century mention black handled knives used in ceremony.

Why a black handle? This does seem to date back to the 'Key of Solomon' book and references to the knife having a black handle and this has perhaps carried on primarily into the

Wiccan tradition. I own two athames, one has a carved grey handle the other is natural brown wood. Neither of them have suffered from not having a black handle! Most knives would originally have been made with a wooden handle because it was the most practical material to work with. One suggestion is that the handle became black due to blood stains from those working magic with them.

And the double edge? Back to the 'Key of Solomon' again, as this seems to feature mostly double edge blades. When I think of swords and daggers, they are double edged, so perhaps it is to align with them?

And what about swords? I think they work in a very similar way to the athame in ritual and magic. However, most Witches I know will have an athame in some form or another, very few of them own a sword. Swords didn't appear in our history until man could create the metal to make one. The first swords were created in bronze, which is quite a soft metal and not really designed for battle. Once iron was discovered swords changed up, and then eventually the Romans made steel swords which was pretty much a game changer.

Swords are expensive, and having used one myself to cast a circle in ritual – they are extremely heavy to wield. Forget just holding one to cast a circle, I would never have the strength to swing one in battle! Perhaps not a tool that most of us use or even consider a working magical tool. I think the sword is more useful in big ceremonial rituals as it carries the grandeur with it.

I have talked about athames with metal blades and wooden handles, but you can create an athame from most materials. Carved stone and bone make for beautiful tools. Or a complete athame made entirely from wood will be wonderful. If you create an athame from wood it would carry the specific energy of the tree that it came from, the same would be true of bone, carrying the energy of that animal within. Go with what works for you. And if you don't want to work with a ceremonial dagger at all, then don't feel that you need to. Witchcraft is a very personal journey, what works for some doesn't always work for others.

Just a quick mention here for the boline. Traditionally a knife with a curved blade used for cutting and harvesting herbs. Whereas the ceremonial athame sports a black handle, this one traditionally has a white handle. The blade to a boline is sharp and sickle shaped. This is a very practical tool. Again, I don't believe it needs to have a white handle, go with what you choose. To be honest I don't use a boline at all. For practical harvesting of herbs and plants a good strong and sharp pair of secateurs seems far better designed for the job at hand.

Invoking and Banishing Pentagrams

You can use a pentagram to invoke or banish the elements in ritual. Each element starts and ends with a different point of the pentagram. The symbols are drawn in the air using your finger, a wand or an athame. As you draw the image, visualise it appearing in the air before you.

To call the element of fire start with your finger/wand/athame at the top of the pentagram and draw a line down to the right point first, then continue back up to draw the rest of the pentagram.

To banish the element of fire, perform the action in reverse, starting from the bottom right point.

To will

In modern Wicca the Witch's Pyramid features the four elements plus that of spirit. It is not actually a physical pyramid but forms the shape of one. Each point represents one of the elements and this can be reflected in the pentagram shape too. Fire represents 'to will'. This is all about you learning the art of focus and visualisation. Your will and intent is the strength behind every spell you cast. If your will is not strong enough then the energy won't be there for your magic to work. It takes time, effort and practise to hone this skill.

Instrument

All stringed instruments are associated with the element of fire, in particular the guitar. I have absolutely no skill with the guitar at all, but there are some very talented players out there. If you don't play a stringed instrument have a look on YouTube for some suitable music. Or listen to some of your favourite bands and the guitar solos.

The Elementals

The Elementals are the energies of nature itself; they are the forces of the elements. They are true energy and have the characteristics of the element they belong to. They can take on any shape, size or form to deal with a particular task.

Elementals can charge us with energy; they can work with us on a physical, mental, emotional and spiritual level. Learning to work with them can tune us in to connect with the energy of nature around us. The Elementals interweave their energy patterns to create and keep all of nature, all of life on our planet. Elementals have nothing to obstruct them, they can move through matter with ease, but they also need to connect with us to help with their own spiritual growth and evolution.

In ancient Greece they were referred to as the kings of the four winds. Ancient Egyptians saw them as four sons of Horus. And the Norse had four dwarves, each one holding up a corner of the world.

In modern Wicca each group of Elementals has a higher being that looks over them, a King. Overseeing the Kings are Archangels. It is quite a hierarchical set up. There are, as you know four elements, so there are four Elementals, four Elemental Kings and four Archangels.

Archangel Michael

Believed to have been the first angel created, Michael is often portrayed as the big boss angel. His name translates as 'He who is like God'. Remember the Bible story where Moses is greeted by a burning bush? Yep, that fire was Michael. He also makes an appearance in several other fire related Bible stories. He is the archangel of fire and the sun, often seen carrying a sword or the scales of justice. He is a defender of those that are deserving and brings protection with him. If you are looking for an archangel to help you achieve your dreams and focus on your goals then this is the dude for the job. I will be completely honest here; I don't work with angels or Archangels at all. But if you are drawn to do so, follow your intuition. However, if you are put off by the thought of angels being Christian, remember that the idea of angels is found in many cultures and they predate Christianity. Basically, angels are universal.

King Djinn

Think warrior type dude with tanned skin, bulging biceps and shiny armour. Well, that's how I think of King Djinn anyway. He has been in a lot of battles, seen it all, done it all and got the severed heads to prove it. He controls the energy and power of life, courage, confidence, your inner strength and transformation of all kinds. He usually appears surrounded by flames, of course, why not? He is direct and doesn't mince his words. He will tell you what he thinks you need to hear, not necessarily what you want, bear that in mind.

Salamanders

Salamanders are the embodiment of Fire. Any flame has the spirit of the fire Elemental within it. They control all fires, all flames, lightning, heat, volcanoes and any explosions.

Don't think of the lizard type creature but a flame as it twists and turns like a serpent.

Fire Elementals create very powerful emotions within us, they put the spark of spiritual ideas into our heads and hearts, they are the power that burns old habits and ideals and recreates new ones, and fire destructs and makes way for the new.

Fire Elementals work with us for healing, they can detox the body. But we must be careful as their energy is very strong and not easy to control (think about a fire getting out of hand and how difficult it is to control). They also use their energy to help our spiritual selves, they work with our spiritual energy, and they also stimulate our faith and enthusiasm. They open us up to psychic insight and perception. Working with the Salamander can help with vitality and loyalty, making you assertive, spiritual and full of aspiration.

Not being connected with your Fire Elemental can cause lack of self-control, restlessness, and burn out, no patience, distrust and pessimism. On a physical level Salamanders aid our circulation and body temperature, assisting our metabolism.

Fire Elemental shapeshifting meditation

Close your eyes and take a few deep breaths. Feel yourself becoming calm and relaxed with each out breath, letting go of all the worries of the day. Feel any tension leave your body as we prepare to shape shift with the element of fire.

Turn now to face the South the direction of the element of fire.

Visualise, feel and sense this element in whatever form is appropriate for you. This could be a flickering candle flame, the crackling of a hearth fire, the heat of the desert, or a blazing bonfire.

Focus on your image and breathe it in, deep down into your abdomen and into your being. Let the element of fire fill your entire body until you feel yourself burn away and you become fire.

Stay with this element for a couple of breaths ... gradually let the fire recede from your body until it is only in your belly, then release it completely with your next out breath.

Take a few deeper breaths now and when you are ready open your eyes.

Welcome back to your human form.

Exercise

Work with the elemental meditation and keep a record of your experiences.

Working with Fire

Bone Magic

In the old days bones and animal parts were used widely for magical purposes. People were hunters they used all the parts of an animal primarily for food and warmth, and the bones for magic.

Now, I do not advocate anyone popping out and hitting a badger over the head with a stick just to use the bones in a spell. However, nature itself provides dead animals and birds and man in his motor car supplies a lot too. Picking up road kill may sound a bit yucky and is not for everyone or the feint hearted but I think of it as honouring the animal, that it's skin and bones will be put to some good use after it has passed away.

The bones themselves are a good way of connecting with the spirit of the animal and working with those energies. I have a magpie skull on my altar as magpie is one of my animal totems; I put it on my altar in honour of the spirit, the bone of the animal works as a vessel for the spirit to reside in within our realm. Animal bones can also be carried in medicine bags to utilise their particular energies. All animal spirits take time to bond with, so don't rush and it is also a nice idea to leave offerings for the animal bones you have found.

You can wear the bones to take on the attributes and power of the animal that they belonged to. A lot of animals are shamanic in nature, enabling you to tap into their ability to travel between worlds. Feathers, animal skins or bones can also be used in shape shifting. The skins can be worn, and the feathers or bones used as jewellery to aid you in taking on the form of the animal.

Ritual tools can also be made from animal bones – rattles for instance, or tie bones to your staff or wand for an added energy boost. And of course, a bone athame would be very magical.

Don't waste the bones from your Sunday dinner either;

chicken bones especially make really good divination sets. And the bones can be used in your magical work. Keep an eye out when you are walking through the woods and fields because you do occasionally find small animal bones, I have one that I believe to be from a rabbit. Antlers that have been naturally shed also make wonderful magical tools. Also, don't forget about insects, they have bones they just wear them on the outside. Watch for dead insects that can be used in magical workings. Please make sure they are dead first…

Cleaning bones

If you want to work with the bones from a road kill animal there are various ways of cleaning the them for use – do a search on Google for tutorials but the basics are: Clean as much of the flesh from the bones as you can, then the bones can be cleaned either by popping them in a jar with fresh water. Put the lid on then leave it for two or three days, change the water for fresh, keep doing this until the flesh has all come away from the bones. You can also do the same thing using biological washing powder and warm water.

Drop the bones into a dish or jar and very carefully pour over a solution of hydrogen peroxide (the chemist has this or failing that purchase hair bleach, which is what I used on my magpie skull) not only does this take the last bits of flesh away from the bone it also bleaches it to a nice colour.

Or bury it…dig a shallow hole in the soil and bury the bones so that Mother Nature's worms and insects can do the cleaning job for you. This takes patience…and you also need to remember where you buried it.

Red Bones

Some cultures have taken to colouring bones with the colour red to create the image of blood and life energy within them. You can do this fairly easily; mix red wine and red ochre together to make a paste and leave it to sit covered in a bowl for a couple of days.

If you can't get red ochre, you can use red brick dust. Apply the paste to the cleaned bones making sure to cover them completely. Wrap the items in plastic to keep the paste moist. Leave for a further twenty-four hours.

If the paste looks like it is drying out give it a spray with water. Remove the paste and allow the bones to dry. You may need to use a soft brush to remove any lingering paste. Don't wash the bones but just wipe with a soft cloth.

Exercise

If you are happy to handle bones do some experimenting with them. Find yourself some bones, just bones from your dinner will be fine. See if you can connect with the energy and make some notes about your experiences with them.

Thorns

Lots of plants have thorns on them; roses, brambles and blackthorn spring to mind and these thorns can be used for magic. Think about what a thorn does, they are protection for the plant, they guard it against predators and they are sharp and defensive. They can pierce, they can cut and they can draw blood. Whilst thorns obviously grow on plants which could be thought of as earth related. I think of thorns as being filled with the element of fire.

Folk lore says that blackthorn thorns were always used to curse but folklore says a lot of things that we have since twisted around to our advantage but if that is the choice you make... thorns (any type) are very good for cursing and hexing spell work, rose thorns work especially well in affairs of a broken heart.

A blackthorn wand with the thorns on is sometimes referred to as a 'black rod' and used in darker magic to cause harm to others. In medieval times it was believed that the Devil pricked the fingers of his followers with thorns from the blackthorn tree.

But thorns also have a positive side and can be used in spell workings for protection and to dispel negative energy.

Long thorns such as those of the blackthorn can be used instead of pins to stick into poppets and also used to carve symbols into candles. Don't forget poppets can be used for all kinds of intent not just hexing they can also be used for healing, love, friendship, protection or whatever use you want really.

Use thorns dipped in ink to write magical petitions or 'fix' magical workings. Use thorns in magic to 'pierce' negative bubbles and break bad cycles that you have gotten into.

Exercise
Find some thorns, preferably at least two different types and work with them. Connect with their energy.

Places
There are certain places and locations that align with the element of fire. If you can take yourself off to visit them to connect that is perfect. If that isn't possible crack out your visualisation skills and meditate to take yourself there.

BBQ
Who doesn't love a BBQ? Well actually I guess that depends on where you are in the world, if it is the UK often BBQs are rained off. My perfect idea of a BBQ is a big ole barnyard one. As my garden is not nearly big enough for that style of affair, here it is in meditation form instead. Find a quiet place where you won't be disturbed and make yourself comfortable. Take a few deep breaths in and out.

As your world around you dissipates you find yourself standing on a dusty patch of earth, surrounded by wooden barns and a huge hayloft.

In the centre is a long row of what looks like half metal barrels lifted up on a framework of stands.

On the other side are several long tables covered with red and white gingham cloths.

People are moving around tipping what looks to be charcoal bricks into each barrel and then lifting large metal grilles on top.

You are in the centre of a big ranch BBQ.

The charcoal is lit in each BBQ barrel and people peer over them poking and adjusting the coals to make sure the fires are lit.

Glasses of refreshment are handed out to everyone and you all talk and laugh with each other.

You accept a glass that is offered to you, the liquid is cool and sweet.

After a while large trays of food are brought out and placed beside each BBQ grill.

You are ushered up to one of the BBQ drums and handed some tools and a tray of food. Encouraging you to cook your own food.

The tray is heavily laden with all kinds of produce, prepped and ready to grill.

You select the items you want to cook and place them on the metal grill above the now smouldering coals.

Each one sizzles and spits and smoke rises from the hot charcoal beneath.

Also on the tray is a tub filled with what looks like a spice mix, open it and take a sniff. It smells sweet and spicy so you sprinkle it over the items on the grill.

Turn the food on the grill with your tongs and watch the spits and listen to the sizzles.

A delicious scent begins to fill the air.

Once your food is cooked to your liking take some off the grill and onto a plate.

Make your way over to a pile of hay bales and sit, making yourself comfortable.

Sit and eat, picking the food up with your fingers, tasting it,

savouring each mouthful and the smoky flavour.
Talk with your fellow diners as you share your food and thoughts with each other.
When you are finished you head back to your BBQ grill.
The coals are now dark and grey, barely smouldering and covered with a powdery ash.
Can you see any symbols or images in the ash or the dying coals?
Think about what it means to you and what the process of cooking your own food and sharing with others means too.

When you are ready, come back to the here and now. Open your eyes and wriggle your fingers and toes.

Bonfire – The Straw Man

There many reasons to have a bonfire, whether it is a small one in your garden to get rid of garden waste or a large group bonfire. In this meditation I take you on a journey to experience a specific bonfire, that of the burning straw man. Find a quiet place where you won't be disturbed and make yourself comfortable. Take a few deep breaths in and out.

As your world around you dissipates you find yourself standing in a field. The sky is dark with a full moon hanging in the sky.
People are moving around you, talking and laughing.
You can hear the distant beating of drums.
Looking around you can see a large round house with smoke snaking up and out of the roof.
People are standing in groups talking and eating.
A group of drummers are entertaining the crowds. Some of the audience are dancing to the beat.
And in the centre of it all, a tall straw figure towers above everything.
You walk towards it to take a closer look.
People are writing on slips of parchment and pushing them into the straw figure.

Someone offers you a slip of parchment and a small piece of charcoal to write with. Explaining you need to write your petition, wish or need.

You take the items and think carefully about what you would like to write.

Take your time, once you have written on your parchment roll it up and move towards the straw figure.

Tucking your petition in between the layers of straw.

Now everyone seems to be moving back and the drumming is getting louder.

A procession is making its way across the field and down towards the straw figure.

People carrying flaming torches lead a row of drummers.

As they reach the straw figure they stop and one of the torch bearers moves close and lights the base of the straw.

Everyone seems to hold their breath.

Until the flames take hold, sparks flying out and loud crackles as the straw gives in to the will of the fire.

You watch as flames begin to lick higher, consuming the straw bit by bit.

A loud crack and part of the figure gives way, crumbling in on itself, the flames leaping victoriously into the space.

Time passes as you watch the straw figure diminish.

And the flames begin to die down.

As the sun begins to rise, peaking over the horizon.

Night becomes day as the straw man becomes ash.

When you are ready, come back to the here and now. Open your eyes and wriggle your fingers and toes.

Desert

Lots and lots of barren space, dusty, dry and often sand as far as the eye can see. Definitely a place for the element of fire. Most of us don't have direct access to a desert, so meditation is the answer. Find a quiet place where you won't be disturbed and make yourself comfortable. Take a few deep breaths in and out.

As your world around you dissipates you find yourself in a barren landscape. Golden white sand as far as you can see in front of you, behind you and in every direction around you.

Above you is a bright blue sky, the sun shining down with all its strength.

But you feel comfortable and look down to see you are wearing loose light weight flowing clothing. Your head too is covered with light fabric to create some shade.

Surveying the landscape there appears to be nothing but sand, until you notice a small wisp of smoke on the horizon, just barely there. You head in that direction.

As you walk you feel the sand beneath your feet and the warmth of the sun on your skin.

The closer you get, the more you can see. The smoke is rising from a small fire created from branches and twigs. A tripod of poles stands over the fire with an iron skillet suspended between.

Then the scent hits your nose, a delicious smell of food being cooked. You realise there is a figure beside the fire, tending to it and turning whatever is on the skillet.

As you approach, they look up and greet you, gesturing for you to sit with them, which you do.

Making yourself comfortable on the cushions and throws on the ground, you feel at ease.

Your host hands you a flask and encourages you to drink from it. The liquid is warm and sweet.

They begin talking to you, telling you about living in the desert and their nomadic lifestyle. What they learn and experience from living on such barren land.

As they are telling you about their adventures the food that has been cooking is ready and they offer you a plate laden with freshly grilled food.

You accept and eat; it is hot and a little spicy but delicious.
Your host asks if you have any questions. Anything that the wisdom
of the desert could help with.
You find yourself talking freely…
Listen carefully to the response.
Take as much time as you need.
When you are ready, thank your host and stand up. Turn and make
your way back, feeling once again the sand beneath your feet and
the sun on your skin.

Slowly and gently come back to this reality, open your eyes and
wriggle your fingers and toes.

Volcano

Obviously, it would be pretty dangerous to go and stand inside
an active volcano. But there are some places in the world that
have dormant volcanoes you can visit. We went to one in
Tenerife many years ago, the overlying experience was that it
smelt of rotten eggs… (it's the sulphur). Amazing if you can visit
one though, if you can't then meditation is the answer. Find a
quiet place where you won't be disturbed and make yourself
comfortable. Take a few deep breaths in and out.

As your world around you dissipates you find yourself standing on
a hill top, with a valley below you and a mountain on the other side.
As you take in your surroundings you notice the mountain across
the valley from you looks a bit different than a usual mountain or
hill top.
The slopes leading up to the peak appear to be dark grey in colour
with no apparent vegetation at all.
As your eyes scan upwards you realise the top of the mountain
appears to be flat, no wait, not flat but a crater.
As you are watching, a wisp of smoke rises up from inside, or is it
steam?

Slowly at first and then more. It is followed by spits and sparks, red and yellow flecks flying up into the air.

Fixed to the spot with awe you watch as the sparks increase and become larger.

Until a huge eruption of lava shoots up into the air and spills over the sides of the crater.

Red hot lava flowing over the edge and making its way down the slopes.

Slinking slowly downwards consuming the sides of the mountain.

Its progress slows and the red dulls now, turning black in places.

A sulphur scent fills the air and you can feel the heat from the volcano even at your safe distance away.

Watch as the lava cools now and begins to crust over and set.

You pause to think about the process of the lava, erupting in anger and cascading down, slowing then cooling to dark ash. How does this equate to any areas in your life?

Ash now fills the air, clouding your view between the mountains.

And the volcano rests, entering its slumber once more.

Watch for a little longer until you can see no more through the ash haze.

And when you are ready come back to the here and now. Open your eyes and wriggled your fingers and toes.

Fireplace

A lot of homes still have a fireplace and large stately homes and castles definitely still have them in place. With sizes ranging from a small space just big enough for a few logs to huge fireplaces large enough to stand in. If you don't have one, then try meditating to experience it. Find a quiet place where you won't be disturbed and make yourself comfortable. Take a few deep breaths in and out.

As your world around you dissipates you find yourself in a large room. The floor beneath you is made from large stone slabs and the walls are hung with heavy detailed tapestries.

In front of you is a huge stone fireplace, so big you could stand up inside it.

On the hearth is a large iron fire basket and grate.

Beside the fireplace is a stack of logs, small kindling, paper and matches.

You shiver and realise it is very cold in this draughty stone room.

Make your way to the fireplace.

Ball up pieces of the paper and place them in the grate.

Pile kindling over them to form a pyre or pyramid shape.

Now use the matches to light the paper. Blowing gently to send the flame upwards to catch the kindling.

Once it takes light, take a look around and notice a large floor cushion and blanket to one side.

Pull them over in front of the fire and make yourself comfortable.

Throw a log onto the flames to keep the fire lit.

Sit quietly and watch the flames dance, their movement and colour flickering and creating shapes.

You see a dish to the other side of you and note it is filled with what looks like dried herbs.

Pick up the dish and smell the herbs, take in the scent and feel of each one.

Ask a question you are seeking an answer for and throw the herbs into the fire.

Watch the flames for any messages, symbols or images.

Ask as many questions as you need and watch for the answers.

Slowly the fire begins to die down.

Watch as the embers glow and transform to ash.

And when you are ready stand up. Slowly and gently come back to this reality. Open your eyes and wriggle your fingers and toes.

Dancing

There are many forms of dance and some of us are better at dancing than others (I am most definitely in the 'dance like no one is watching' category). But there is a freedom that comes with allowing the beat of music to take over your body. If you can, do let yourself succumb to the rhythm on occasion, it can be incredibly rewarding. Even if your body is less willing than your spirit, you can use the power of meditation to create that feeling of energy. Find a quiet place where you won't be disturbed and make yourself comfortable. Take a few deep breaths in and out.

As your world around you dissipates you find yourself standing outside a set of tall modern wooden double doors.

Behind you, voices are approaching with excited chatter and bubbly laughter.

Turning, you are greeted by a group of people dressed in loose, comfortable clothing. All appear to be eager to enter through the doors you are standing in front of.

They usher you in with them as the doors swing open.

Inside is a large room with a polished wooden floor and mirrors that stretch from floor to ceiling on each wall.

The other people move to stand in the centre of the floor, giving themselves space.

They signal for you to join them, so you move into a free space, wondering what will happen next.

And then the music starts…

A slow steady beat at first…listen to it…feel it…allow it to wash over you.

The others in the room begin to move in time with the rhythm.

There doesn't appear to be set pattern of movements. Everyone is interpreting the music themselves. Each one moving differently.

You feel the impulse to move with the beat yourself. You feel free to move as you wish.

This is virtual, there are no physical restrictions, you move

completely freely, your body moving with ease.
The pace of the music picks up and you find yourself moving along with it.
Totally free to go with the ebb and flow of the music.
Go with it...
Eventually the beat begins to slow down and you move in time with it.
Until the music gradually comes to a stop.
You feel exhilarated, enthusiastic and fired up.
Someone hands you a cool drink, which you receive gratefully.
Take a moment now to sit down on the floor and look at your reflection in the large mirrors.
This is you; passionate, full of energy, renewed, revitalised and filled with the spark of inspiration and accomplishment.
Use this energy to channel into something positive.
When you are ready, stand up from your seated position. Thank the other participants for allowing you to join them.
Make your way back to the doors and step out into the fresh air.

Slowly and gently come back to this reality. Open your eyes and wriggle your fingers and toes.

Creativity

Creativity comes in many forms, it can be artistic such as painting or drawing but also encompasses sewing, knitting, sculpting, carving and any number of creative outlets. If you have the ability and the materials to tap into your creativity it is a wonderful way to express yourself. If you don't have that ability or maybe you haven't ever tried, meditation is a good way to start. Unleash your inner artist. Find a quiet place where you won't be disturbed and make yourself comfortable. Take a few deep breaths in and out.

As your world around you dissipates you find yourself in an alleyway in what looks to be part of an old city. In front of you is a battered and worn door with all the old paint peeling off.

You push the door open.

Inside is a large room with a very high ceiling.

The walls are painted a crisp white and the floor is old worn floorboards, marked, scuffed and covered in what look like splatters of paint.

In the centre of the room is a large easel on which stands a huge blank canvas.

Beside it is an old wood table laid out with tubes of paint in a rainbow of colours. Beside them is an old glass jar filled with paint brushes of all sizes.

You are alone, the room is empty, but the canvas is drawing you in.

Investigate the table, pick up all the paints and look at the colours.

Feel the weight of the brushes in your hand.

Touch the blank canvas, run your hands across the empty space.

Now is the time to fire up your creativity.

Pick up a brush and one of the paints and release your art…

You have free rein, use whatever colours you feel drawn to, whatever brushes, palette knives or even your hands.

Create your masterpiece…

When you are done, take a step back and admire your work.

What do you see? What does it mean to you?

Pull up a chair that you see in the corner of the room, place it in front of your artwork.

Take a seat and look at the image you have created. Spend some time studying it.

When you are ready stand up and take a last look at your art.

Turn and make your way back to the door and step out into the alleyway.

Slowly and gently come back to this reality. Open your eyes and wriggle your fingers and toes.

Restaurant Kitchen

What can be more fiery than the centre of a busy restaurant kitchen? The heat from the appliances and the energy raised from the hustle and bustle of chefs and cooks preparing food for lots of hungry customers. If you don't fancy the heat of a real restaurant kitchen, let's delve into your imagination instead. Find a quiet place where you won't be disturbed and make yourself comfortable. Take a few deep breaths in and out.

As your world around you dissipates you find yourself in amongst the hustle and noise of a restaurant kitchen.

Stainless steel surfaces, cookers and appliances surround you.

The air is loud with the noise of people busy cooking and shouting orders at each other.

And the scent hits your nose…

Spices and herbs, cardamom, ginger, turmeric, fenugreek and cinnamon.

The delights of lots of different curries, rice dishes and Indian cuisine fills the air.

You are handed a pan and ushered towards a work station.

In front of you are small dishes filled with spices of all colours and textures.

A board filled with vegetables, some you recognise, others are unknown to you. They are all prepped and ready to cook.

Place your pan on the stove top and light the flame beneath.

Add a dash of oil and let it start to warm.

Now throw in a pinch of spice from each pot.

Each one sizzles as it hits the hot oil and each one has a different and very distinctive scent.

Stir the pan and add in the vegetables.

Breathe in the spicy air and listen to the busy sounds of the kitchen.

So much noise and energy as the kitchen staff go about their duties.

Keep stirring your vegetables until they look ready then take the pan from the heat.

Use a fork or a spoon and take a taste of your spicy creation.
What can you taste?
What flavours?
What textures?
Thank about the process that has taken place to create a meal.
Eat until you are full.
Now take a last look around the kitchen and take in the fast, positive
energy that has been created here.

When you are ready slowly and gently come back to this reality.
Open your eyes and wriggle your fingers and toes.

Fire Walk

If you ever get the chance to take part in a fire walk, I would
encourage you to do so. It is a very spiritual and energising
experience. Until then, here is another option in the form of
meditation. Find a quiet place where you won't be disturbed and
make yourself comfortable. Take a few deep breaths in and out.

As your world around you dissipates you find yourself in a clearing
in a woodland. It is dusk but the weather is warm.
You see people bustling about in the centre of the clearing.
Watch as they seem to be tending to something on the ground. Move
closer to investigate.
It is a long narrow strip on the woodland floor.
Edged with small rocks it looks like hot coals, burning embers
glowing in the dim light.
You watch for a moment as they prepare the coals.
Beside you is a round wooden hut with a straw roof, so you make
your way inside.
There are others in here, all seated around the edge.
You are handed a small mug filled with liquid and directed to take
a seat.
Make yourself comfortable and begin to sip your drink. It is warm

and tastes of herbs and spices.

Then a drum beat begins, slowly and steadily.

A voice begins to speak, it asks you to prepare yourself for transformation.

Think about what you would like to release from your life, things you want to let go of. Habits, thought patterns, old emotions...

And then what changes you want to make in your life, your way of thinking or your routine...

Take your time...

Then you are led out of the hut.

It is night time now and the dark sky above holds just a slither of moon.

The pathway of coals is lit either side by rows of flaming torches. The embers glowing and smouldering in the dark.

One by one the others in front of you take off their shoes and socks and step onto the fire walk.

Moving quickly but steadily from one end across the coals to step off the other side, amongst cheers from those watching.

And now it is your turn.

Take off your shoes and socks and stand at the edge of the fire walk. Take a deep breath and release any doubts.

Step onto the coals, one foot in front of the other, moving steadily across towards the end.

Each step allows you to release that which no longer serves you.

Hold on to any thoughts, images of insights that come to you as you cross the coals.

And then you are at the other end, refreshed, energised and feeling lighter and brighter.

People cheer and then hug you as you step away from the end of the fire walk.

You move to one side and sit down on the grass. Quietly absorbing your experience and watching others as they take their journeys of transformation across the coals.

When you are ready you stand up, take one last look at the fire walk and make your way back to the edge of the clearing.

When you are ready slowly and gently come back to this reality. Open your eyes and wriggle your fingers and toes.

Sunrise

One of the most beautiful experiences out in Mother Nature is to watch a sunrise. But with our busy lives not everyone can get to see one on a regular basis. It is a very refreshing and energising event. Find a quiet place where you won't be disturbed and make yourself comfortable. Take a few deep breaths in and out.

As your world around you dissipates you find yourself standing on soft white sand, the sky above you is dark, the night sky.
In front of you is the ocean, inky black as the waves gently crash onto the shore.
Just on the horizon you can see a glimpse of light, dawn is on the way and the sun is making preparation to rise.
Ahead you can just make out some rocks, so you walk towards them. As you reach the base you notice a blanket laid out with some cushions.
You sit down and make yourself comfortable.
Then you see a flask propped up against the rocks. You open it to discover warm hot chocolate, so you pour yourself a cup.
Sipping your hot chocolate, you sit and look out towards the sea.
Spend some time watching as the sun begins to rise above the horizon.
The light reflects on the water as it moves upwards, reaching for the skies.
The sky behind it creates a beautiful palette of warm colours; oranges, yellows and pinks.
As the sun rises above the horizon think about the things you would like to manifest in your life.
Take as much time as you want, enjoy the sunrise.

And begin to feel the warmth the sun brings to your skin.
Feel the energy of the sun on your face, your arms and your body.
Soak up the positive solar energy.
The sun is now fully showing its golden face and you feel warm and energised.
Stand up now and face the sun, throw both your arms up into the air and stand for a moment. Welcome the sun and send your gratitude for the energy it provides.
Listen for any messages it may have for you…
When you are ready, bring your arms back down and turn away.

Slowly and gently come back to this reality. Open your eyes and wriggle your fingers and toes.

Blacksmith

A very honoured and ancient tradition is that of the blacksmith. I also think there is a lot of magic attached to this creative art. The smithy is a place where fire meets water and creativity happens. Find a quiet place where you won't be disturbed and make yourself comfortable. Take a few deep breaths in and out.

As your world around you dissipates you find yourself standing outside an old stone building with a dirt track running past.
Listen carefully and you can hear a hammering noise.
Walk around the building, following the dirt track.
To find large wooden doors thrown wide open. Inside is a blacksmith at work.
He is hammering a piece of metal on his anvil.
A large fire is burning fiercely behind him. He takes the metal and pushes it into the heart of the fire and holds it there. Bringing it out again the metal glowing red hot.
He places it on the anvil and continues to hammer.
Then he dips the metal into a large bucket of water beside him, sending up clouds of steam into the air.

You stand and watch, fascinated as he manipulates the metal with heat, the energy of his hammer and the balance of cold water and steam.

What is he making?

He continues at his work as you watch and see what he is fashioning from the metal.

And then he seems to have finished and holds the item up in the air, offering it to you.

The item is important and symbolic to you.

The blacksmith asks if you would like to create something.

He hands you a new piece of metal and you hold it with the tools he provides.

He shows you step by step how to place it in the depths of the flames to heat it.

Then how to hit it and mould it into shape, dipping into the cold water when necessary.

Take your time and learn from him…

Feel the energy of the metal and the heat from the fire, this is transformation at its base level.

Spend as much time as you want or need working with the metal and the fire…

When you are ready, what is your finished creation and what does it mean to you?

Thank the blacksmith for his help and guidance.

Walk back out and around the building to where you began.

Slowly and gently come back to this reality. Open your eyes and wriggle your fingers and toes.

Exercise
Take a look at the fire places mentioned here. Do some research in your local area and see how many of these types of places you can find or even visit. Keep notes on your experiences.

Practical Fire Elements

Herbs and Plants

Each plant has an association or correspondence with one of the elements. Often it is based upon the magical or medicinal properties of the plant. You can work with the plant in meditation or use the actual item as an ingredient in incense or spell work. Here is a basic list of plants and herbs that correspond to the element of fire to get you started:

Anemone
Anemone Magical Properties:
Protection, healing, health
Ruling planet – Mars
Element – Fire
Gender – Masculine

Angelica
Angelica Magical Properties:
Protection, healing, exorcism, divination, prosperity, luck, hex breaking, courage
Ruling planet – Sun, Venus
Sign – Gemini, Cancer, Leo, Libra
Element – Fire
Gender – Masculine

Ash
Ash Magical Properties:
Protection, prosperity, dispels negativity, improves health, sea magic, dreams, love, intuition
Ruling planet – Sun and Neptune
Element – Fire and Water
Gender – Masculine

Betony
Betony Magical Properties:
Love, purification, clarity, protection, anti intoxication, nightmares, anti depression, memory, stress relief
Ruling planet – Jupiter
Sign – Gemini, Sagittarius
Element – Fire
Gender – Masculine

Blackthorn
Blackthorn Magical Properties:
Protection, exorcism, divination, healing
Ruling planet – Saturn and Mars
Sign – Scorpio
Element – Fire
Gender – Masculine

Buttercup
Buttercup Magical Properties:
Abundance, ancient wisdom, divination, protection, psychic abilities
Ruling planet – Sun
Sign – Capricorn
Element – Fire
Gender – Masculine

Carnation
Carnation Magical Properties:
Healing, strength, protection, release, courage
Ruling planet – Sun
Element – Fire
Gender – Masculine

Cedar
Cedar Magical Properties:
Purification, money, protection, Goddess
Ruling planet – Sun, Jupiter
Sign – Sagittarius
Element – Fire
Gender – Masculine

Celandine
Celandine Magical Properties:
Happiness, protection, release, escape, legal matters
Ruling planet – Sun
Element – Fire
Gender – Masculine

Chrysanthemum
Chrysanthemum Magical Properties:
Longevity, spirituality, protection
Ruling planet – Sun
Element – Fire
Gender – Masculine

Cinquefoil
Cinquefoil Magical Properties:
Protection, dreams, divination, magic, love, hex breaking
Ruling planet – Jupiter, Mercury
Sign – Taurus, Gemini
Element – Fire
Gender – Masculine

Cleavers
Cleavers Magical Properties:
Commitment, tenacity, relationships, love, binding
Ruling planet – Saturn

Element – Fire
Gender – Feminine

Copal
Copal Magical Properties:
Purification, love, protection.
Ruling planet – Sun, Jupiter
Sign – Capricorn
Element – Fire
Gender – Masculine

Dragon's Blood
Dragon's Blood Magical Properties:
Power, protection, love, happiness, dragon magic
Ruling planet – Mars
Sign – Aries
Element – Fire
Gender – Masculine

Flax
Flax Magical Properties:
Knot magic, money, protection, healing
Ruling planet – Mercury, Venus
Element – Fire
Gender – Masculine

Frankincense
Frankincense Magical Properties:
Purification, spirituality, relaxation, focus, love, abundance
Ruling planet – Sun
Sign – Aries, Leo, Aquarius
Element – Fire
Gender – Masculine

Gorse
Gorse Magical Properties:
Money, protection
Ruling planet – Mars
Element – Fire
Gender – Masculine

Hawthorn
Hawthorn Magical Properties:
Happiness, fertility, love, protection, purification, forgiveness, faeries, hope
Ruling planet – Mars, Venus
Sign – Sagittarius
Element – Fire
Gender – Masculine

Heliotrope
Heliotrope Magical Properties:
Dreams, spirituality, exorcism, protection, forgiveness, abundance
Ruling planet – Sun
Sign – Leo
Element – Fire
Gender – Masculine

Holly
Holly Magical Properties:
Protection, luck, dreams, balance, success
Ruling planet – Mars, Saturn
Element – Fire
Gender – Masculine

Hyssop
Hyssop Magical Properties:

Purification, protection, healing
Ruling planet – Jupiter, Moon
Sign – Cancer
Element – Fire
Gender – Masculine

Juniper
Juniper Magical Properties:
Love, exorcism, healing, protection, justice, stolen items, purification, psychic powers, clarity
Ruling planet – Sun, Jupiter, Moon
Sign – Aries
Element – Fire
Gender – Masculine

Lovage
Lovage Magical Properties:
Protection, love
Ruling planet – Sun, Moon
Sign – Taurus
Element – Fire
Gender – Masculine

Mandrake
Mandrake Magical Properties:
Protection, love, prosperity
Ruling planet – Mercury
Sign – Taurus, Cancer, Virgo
Element – Fire
Gender – Masculine

Marigold
Marigold Magical Properties:
Psychic powers, dreams, protection, luck, happiness, gossip

Ruling planet – Sun
Sign – Leo
Element – Fire
Gender – Masculine

Mullein
Mullein Magical Properties:
Protection, nightmares, centring
Ruling planet – Saturn, Mercury
Sign – Aquarius
Element – Fire
Gender – Feminine

Nettle
Nettle Magical Properties:
Healing, protection, lust, money, exorcism.
Ruling planet – Mars
Sign – Scorpio, Aries
Element – Fire
Gender – Masculine

Oak
Oak Magical Properties:
Healing, health, protection, money, fertility, luck, strength, vitality, power
Ruling planet – Sun, Jupiter, Mars
Sign – Sagittarius
Element – Fire, Water
Gender – Masculine

Pennyroyal
Pennyroyal Magical Properties:
Strength, protection, peace, initiation, Goddess, business
Ruling planet – Mars, Venus

Sign – Scorpio, Libra
Element – Fire
Gender – Masculine

Peony
Peony Magical Properties:
Exorcism, protection, luck, happiness, blessings
Ruling planet – Sun
Element – Fire
Gender – Masculine

Pine
Pine Magical Properties:
Centring, focus, Dragon magic, protection, truth, abundance, purification, fertility, healing
Ruling planet – Mars, Saturn
Sign – Capricorn
Element – Air, Fire
Gender – Masculine

Rowan
Rowan Magical Properties:
Psychic powers, power, success, protection, love, spirituality, faeries, divination, healing, inspiration
Ruling planet – Sun, Mercury
Sign – Sagittarius
Element – Fire
Gender – Masculine

Rue
Rue Magical Properties:
Protection, health, healing, purification, balance, clarity, anxiety, hex breaking
Ruling planet – Mars, Sun

Sign – Leo
Element – Fire
Gender – Masculine

St John's Wort
Saint John's Wort Magical Properties:
Protection, health, strength, love, divination, happiness, abundance, truth
Ruling planet – Sun
Sign – Aquarius, Libra
Element – Fire
Gender – Masculine

Snapdragon
Snapdragon Magical Properties:
Dragon magic, divination, Elementals, protection, hexes, truth, sleep, nightmares
Ruling planet – Mars
Sign – Gemini
Element – Fire
Gender – Masculine

Sunflower
Sunflower Magical Properties:
Wishes, fertility, truth, integrity, luck, protection, loyalty, happiness
Ruling planet – Sun
Sign – Leo
Element – Fire
Gender – Masculine

Thistle
Thistle Magical Properties:
Protection, healing, exorcism, hex breaking, spirit

Ruling planet – Mars, Jupiter
Element – Fire
Gender – Masculine

Tobacco
Tobacco Magical Properties:
Purification, travel, protection
Ruling planet – Mars
Element – Fire
Gender – Masculine

Walnut
Walnut Magical Properties:
Wishes, mental powers, clarity, fertility
Ruling planet – Sun
Element – Fire
Gender – Masculine

Witch Hazel
Witch Hazel Magical Properties:
Protection, divining, balance, grief
Ruling planet – Sun, Saturn
Sign – Capricorn
Element – Fire
Gender – Masculine

Woodruff
Woodruff Magical Properties:
Protection, money, balance, justice
Ruling planet – Mars
Element – Fire
Gender – Masculine

Wormwood
Wormwood Magical Properties:
Vengeance, attack magic, protection, divination, dreams, meditation, psychic powers
Ruling planet – Mars, Moon
Sign – Cancer, Scorpio
Element – Fire
Gender – Masculine

Incense

Incense can be a loose mixture burnt on charcoal or by lighting incense cones and sticks. Incense is used to clear negative energy, create sacred space, complement spell work or add energy to a ritual. If you can't use incense for health reasons you could try using essential oil on a burner or scented candles. I often pop loose incense onto the top of an oil burner with a tea light underneath. The heat warms the blend and disperses the scent but doesn't give off any smoke. Incense is used frequently to cleanse, whether it is by passing the item through the smoke of the incense itself or by using incense to smudge something – your home, your body or an item. The power of the smoke cleanses and purifies. Loose incense can also be used in spell pouches and witch bottles but also to draw sigils or symbols with.

I start with a tree resin base such as frankincense or copal. Add in something woody to help it burn longer and then dried herbs and spices. To boost the scent, you can add a few drops of essential oil to the mixture.

Some fire element incense blends
Use equal parts of each ingredient.

Fire incense #1
Bay

Black pepper
Cinnamon
Frankincense

Fire incense #2
Cinnamon
Copal
Cumin
Ginger
Nutmeg

Fire incense #3
Rosemary
Dragon's blood resin
Juniper
Cedar

Fire incense #4
Clove
Frankincense
Coriander seed
Marigold

Exercise
Keep a note of any blends that you create and write up how each one worked. It is useful to keep a record for future blends.

Essential Oils
Essential oils have been used for thousands of years in religious ceremonies, for anointing, filling a room with fragrance, in foods and perfumes and for healing and well-being. When purchasing essential oils do make sure they are pure and not mixed with chemicals or 'watered down'. Some of the oils can be expensive but remember that you only use a few drops at a time so they

will last. An essential oil is a concentrated essence of the plant. The oil is extracted from either the seeds, the peel, the resin, leaves, roots, bark or flowers.

Oil blends are useful for dressing candles for spell work, pick a corresponding oil to your intent and rub the candle with the oil. Or adding to your own bath water for a ritual bath or using to anoint yourself before ritual. Oil blends can also be added to an oil burner, I pop a piece of wax into the top first then add the oil, it stops it from burning. Please test a drop or two on a small area of your skin before you go slapping on loads of oil, just in case you are allergic to it. NEVER put essential oil straight onto your skin, always mix it into a base oil first.

A useful method for breathing in essential oils is to create your oil blend then add it to a jar containing a couple of tablespoons of coarse sea salt. Mix together and pop a lid on the jar. Then when you feel the need, open the jar and take a couple of deep breaths.

Oil blends are easy to make, and you can use any type of base oil such as almond oil, jojoba oil, apricot kernel oil, coconut oil, even olive oil. Then add a few drops of essential oil in whatever blends you want. If you are experimenting with blends, I would suggest using pieces of card to test the scent on first. Put a drop of each essential oil on a small slip of card (or paper towel) add the next oil and sniff to see if you like it, then add the next drop etc. Then you won't end up ruining a whole bottle of base oil by adding in random essential oils.

For a blend to use in an oil burner, bath or diffuser you can create a blend without using a base oil. Any blend you are intending to use on your skin for anointing or massage NEEDS to be diluted with a base oil. As a general rule of thumb, I would use 10ml of base oil to 20-25 drops of essential oil.

Some fire essential oil blends

Fire essential oil blend #1
1 part ginger
2 parts grapefruit
2 parts orange
1 part basil

Fire essential oil blend #2
2 parts cinnamon
1 part clove
1 part fennel
1 part pine

Fire essential oil blend #3
1 part cedar
1 part pine
1 part juniper
2 parts frankincense

Fire essential oil blend #4
2 parts dragon's blood
1 part cinnamon
1 part ginger

Exercise
Keep a note of any blends that you create and write up how each one worked. It is useful to keep a record for future blends.

Magical Food
Just as each plant or herb has magical properties, so does food. Use them as offerings, eat to absorb the magic or use in spell working. Here are some foods that correspond to the element of fire:

Artichoke
Artichoke Magical Properties:
Protection, growth, passion, strength, courage
Ruling planet – Mars
Element – Fire
Gender – Masculine/Feminine

Asparagus
Asparagus Magical Properties:
Passion, sex, cleansing, healing
Ruling planet – Mars, Jupiter
Element – Fire
Gender – Masculine (well it wouldn't be anything else really
would it?)

Basil
Basil Magical Properties:
Wealth, money, prosperity, love, exorcism, protection,
happiness, peace
Ruling planet – Mars
Element – Fire
Gender – masculine

Bay
Bay Magical Properties:
Protection, purification, strength, power, healing, creativity,
spirituality, psychic powers
Ruling planet – Sun
Element – Fire
Gender – Masculine

Beef
Beef Magical Properties:
Power, fertility

Element – Fire, Earth
Gender – Masculine

Beer
Beer Magical Properties:
Dreams, purification, offerings
Ruling planet – Mars
Element – Fire
Gender – Masculine

Blackberries
Blackberries Magical Properties:
Prosperity, protection, fertility, Faerie
Ruling planet – Venus
Element – Water, Fire, Earth
Gender – Feminine

Black pepper
Black Pepper Magical Properties:
Protection, exorcism, jealousy, negativity, strength, confidence, gossip
Ruling planet – Mars
Element – Fire
Gender – Masculine

Carrot
Carrot Magical Properties:
Clarity, fertility, passion
Ruling planet – Mars
Element – Fire
Gender – Masculine

Cashew
Cashew Magical Properties:

Prosperity, energy
Ruling planet – Sun
Element – Fire, Earth
Gender – Feminine

Celery
Celery Magical Properties:
Clarity, passion, peace
Ruling planet – Mercury
Element – Fire, Water, Air
Gender – Masculine

Chestnut
Chestnut Magical Properties:
Strength, success, prosperity, abundance, fertility
Ruling planet – Jupiter
Element – Fire
Gender – Masculine

Chicken
Chicken Magical Properties:
Healing, divination, prosperity, luck, fertility
Element – Fire
Gender – feminine

Chillies
Chillies Magical Properties:
Creativity, energy, power, protection, passion, hex breaking
Ruling planet – Mars
Element – Fire
Gender – Masculine

Chives
Chives Magical Properties:

Exorcism, negative energy, bad habits, protection
Ruling planet – Mars
Element – Fire
Gender – Masculine

Chocolate
Chocolate Magical Properties:
Prosperity, positive energy, happiness, love
Ruling planet – Mars
Element – Fire
Gender – Feminine

Cinnamon
Cinnamon Magical Properties:
Success, healing, power, psychic powers, protection, love, focus, lust, spirituality, changes
Ruling planet – Sun
Element – Fire
Gender – Masculine

Clove
Clove Magical Properties:
Love, money, exorcism, clarity, protection, abundance, repels negativity, prevents gossip, stress relief, truth
Ruling planet – Jupiter
Element – Fire
Gender – Masculine

Coffee
Coffee Magical Properties:
Energy, clarity, divination
Ruling planet – Mars
Element – Fire, Water
Gender – Feminine

Coriander
Coriander Magical Properties:
Health, healing, peace, love, release, wealth, protection, negativity
Ruling planet – Mars
Element – Fire
Gender – Masculine

Corn
Corn Magical Properties:
Abundance, luck, prosperity, offerings, fertility
Ruling planet – Sun
Element – Fire, Earth
Gender – Feminine

Cranberry
Cranberry Magical Properties:
Protection, emotions, communication
Ruling planet – Mars
Element – Water, Fire
Gender – Feminine

Cumin
Cumin Magical Properties:
Exorcism, protection, anti-theft, fidelity, lust, peace, love, abundance, success
Ruling planet – Mars
Element – Fire
Gender – Masculine

Curry
Curry Magical Properties:
Energy, passion
Ruling planet – Mars

Element – Fire
Gender – Masculine

Curry leaves
Curry Leaves Magical Properties:
Protection
Ruling planet – Mars
Element – Fire
Gender – Masculine

Eggs
Eggs Magical Properties:
Fertility, creation, life, new beginnings, divination
Element – Water, Earth, Air, Fire
Gender – Masculine/Feminine

Endive
Endive Magical Properties:
Lust, love
Ruling planet – Jupiter
Element – Air, Fire
Gender – Masculine

Fennel
Fennel Magical Properties:
Purification, protection, healing
Ruling planet – Mercury
Element – Fire
Gender – Masculine

Figs
Figs Magical Properties:
Meditation, love, fertility, divination
Ruling planet – Jupiter

Element – Air, Fire
Gender – Masculine/Feminine

Game
Game Magical Properties:
Fidelity, divination, power, energy
Element – Fire, Air, Earth, Water
Gender – Masculine

Garlic
Garlic Magical Properties:
Healing, protection, hex breaking, negative energies, lust, strength, courage, depression
Ruling planet – Mars
Element – Fire
Gender – Masculine

Ginger
Ginger Magical Properties:
Healing, power, love, passion, success, prosperity, protection
Ruling planet – Mars
Element – Fire
Gender – Masculine

Grapefruit
Grapefruit Magical Properties:
Happiness, spirit work, purification, depression, energy
Ruling planet – Jupiter, Sun
Element – Fire, Water
Gender – Feminine

Horseradish
Horseradish Magical Properties:
Protection, energy, purification, passion

Ruling planet – Mars
Element – Fire
Gender – Masculine

Lamb
Lamb Magical Properties:
Caring, nurture, new life, beginnings, spring, fertility
Element – Fire, Earth
Gender – Masculine

Leeks
Leeks Magical Properties:
Purification, protection, love
Ruling planet – Mars
Element – Fire
Gender – Masculine

Lemongrass
Lemongrass Magical Properties:
Faerie magic, happiness, divination, ceremonial, knowledge,
shape shifting
Ruling planet – Mercury
Element – Fire
Gender – Masculine

Lime
Lime Magical Properties:
Purification, love, healing, protection, energy
Ruling planet –Sun
Element – Fire
Gender – Masculine

Liver
Liver Magical Properties:

Courage, power and the magical energies of the specific animal it came from
Element – Fire

Lobster
Lobster Magical Properties:
Sea magic, power, courage
Element – Water, Fire
Gender – Masculine

Mango
Mango Magical Properties:
Spirituality, love, fertility, passion
Ruling planet – Mars
Element – Fire, Air
Gender – Feminine

Mustard
Mustard Magical Properties:
Clarity, psychic abilities, protection, astral travel, faith, success
Ruling planet – Mars
Element – Fire
Gender – Masculine

Nutmeg
Nutmeg Magical Properties:
Money, luck, fidelity, protection
Ruling planet – Jupiter
Element – Fire
Gender – Masculine

Olives
Olives Magical Properties:

Spirituality, integrity, passion, fertility, healing, peace, protection, luck
Ruling planet – Sun
Element – Fire, Air
Gender – Masculine

Orange
Orange Magical Properties:
Love, happiness, uplifting, generosity, purification, clarity, energy, fidelity
Ruling planet – Sun
Element – Fire
Gender – Masculine

Paprika
Paprika Magical Properties:
Creativity, energy
Ruling planet – Mars
Element – Fire
Gender –Masculine

Pineapple
Pineapple Magical Properties:
Chastity, protection, luck, prosperity, healing
Ruling planet – Sun
Element – Fire
Gender – Masculine

Pomegranate
Pomegranate Magical Properties:
Growth, fertility, wishes, death, rebirth, new beginnings
Ruling planet – Mercury
Element – Fire, Earth
Gender – Masculine

Pork
Pork Magical Properties:
Strength, fertility, prosperity, luck, longevity
Element – Fire
Gender – Masculine

Radish
Radish Magical Properties:
Protection, passion, happiness
Ruling planet – Mars
Element – Fire
Gender – Masculine

Rosemary
Rosemary Magical Properties:
Protection, love, lust, mental powers, exorcism, purification, healing, sleep
Ruling planet – Sun
Element – Fire
Gender – Masculine

Saffron
Saffron Magical Properties:
Happiness, energy, psychic powers, healing, fertility
Ruling planet – Sun
Element – Fire
Gender – Masculine

Sesame
Sesame Magical Properties:
Prosperity, protection, energy, strength, secrets
Ruling planet – Sun
Element – Fire, Earth
Gender – Masculine

Sunflower Seeds
Sunflower Seeds Magical Properties:
Fertility, sun magic, strength, courage, happiness, prosperity, confidence
Ruling planet – Sun
Element – Fire
Gender – Masculine

Tea (black)
Tea Magical Properties:
Meditation, courage, strength, prosperity
Ruling planet – Sun
Element – Fire
Gender – Masculine

Turkey
Turkey Magical Properties:
Motivation, clarity, focus, celebration
Element – Fire, Air
Gender – Masculine

Turmeric
Turmeric Magical Properties:
Purification, protection, peace
Ruling planet – Mars
Element – Fire, Air
Gender – Feminine

Vinegar
Vinegar Magical Properties:
Fire energy, protection
Ruling planet – Mars
Element – Fire
Gender – Masculine

Walnut
Walnut Magical Properties:
Wishes, mental powers, clarity, fertility
Ruling planet – Sun
Element – Fire
Gender – Masculine

Watercress
Watercress Magical Properties:
Clarity, protection, fertility
Ruling planet – Mars
Element – Fire, Water
Gender – Feminine

Wine
Wine Magical Properties:
Spirituality, offerings, happiness, love
Ruling planet – Sun (red wine), Moon (white wine)
Element – Earth, Fire
Gender – Masculine and Feminine

Exercise
Keep a record of which foods you use in magical workings and what the result was. It is useful to refer back to for future spells.

Fire Recipes
Fire gets involved whenever you use the oven or the hob to cook your food, but there are certain ingredients that really embody the element of fire. Here are some of my favourites, all of them are obviously based around cake and cookies, because, well why wouldn't they be?

Blackberry Jam Cake
A very lovely friend gifted me a jar of her homemade blackberry

jam and it is delicious. But I thought I might add some to a cake, this is the result. Quite possibly one of my most favourite cakes ever... You could of course use any flavour of jam.

500g/17.6 oz plain/all-purpose flour
1 teaspoon ground cinnamon
1 teaspoon ground allspice
1 teaspoon grated nutmeg
1/2 teaspoon ground cloves
1 teaspoon baking powder
225g/8 oz butter, softened
300g/10.5 oz dark brown sugar
1/2 teaspoon salt
3 large eggs
350g/12.4 oz blackberry jam
200ml/7 fl oz buttermilk (if you don't have buttermilk use regular milk with a teaspoon of lemon juice added)

For the icing:
100g/3.5 oz dark brown sugar
55g/2 oz butter
60g/2 oz plain yogurt
2 tablespoons plain/all-purpose flour
1/2 teaspoon vanilla extract

Preheat your oven to 350F/180C/Gas 4.

Grease and flour a large bundt pan. If you don't have a bundt tin you can place an empty tin can in the centre of a large cake tin.

Cream the sugar and butter together until light and fluffy.

Pop the flour, cinnamon, allspice, nutmeg, cloves, salt and baking powder into a separate large bowl.

Now add the eggs a little at a time to the creamed butter/sugar mixture, whisking in between. Add the jam and mix. Now add the dry ingredients alternately with the buttermilk, a little at a time until combined.

Pour the batter into the prepared tin.

Bake in the oven for about an hour, until a skewer comes out clean.

Turn out from the tin and allow to cool.

To make the icing, pop all the ingredients into a saucepan. Set it over a medium low heat and bring to the boil, stirring continuously. Keep it on a gentle boil, whisking until the mixture thickens, this will take about five minutes or so. Remove from the heat and allow to cool slightly. Then spoon over the cake.

Black Pepper Butter Cookies

I know this sounds totally bonkers, but the addition of black pepper gives a warmth to the cookie. Pre ground pepper works best, you can use freshly ground black pepper but you need to make sure it is very fine. You don't want lumps of black peppercorn in the cookies!

330g/10.6 oz plain/all-purpose flour
200g/7 oz sugar
225g/8 oz butter, softened
1 large egg
1 teaspoon baking powder
1 teaspoon vanilla extract
1 level teaspoon finely ground black pepper
Tablespoon of sugar

Preheat your oven to 350F/180C/Gas 4.

Pop all the ingredients except the tablespoon of sugar into a large bowl and mix. If you have a food mixer it is much easier.

Once the dough has come together make 1 inch balls and place them on a large baking sheet. Leave space because they will spread.

Using the base of a drinking glass dip it into the sugar then use it to squash each dough ball on the baking sheet. It will flatten them into even cookie shapes. Re-dip in the sugar before flattening each ball.

Bake for 12-13 minutes until the edges are lightly browned.

Chocolate Carrot Cake
Carrots and chocolate in a cake, yep, 'tis a marriage made in heaven, trust me.

> 300g/10.6 oz grated carrots
> 400g/14 oz sugar
> 300ml/10.1 fl oz vegetable oil
> 4 large eggs
> 300g/10.6 oz plain/all-purpose flour
> 60g/2.1 oz cocoa powder
> 1 teaspoon baking powder
> ½ teaspoon salt
>
> Frosting
> 200g butter, softened
> 100g dark chocolate, melted
> 350g icing sugar

Line two 8" baking tins with baking parchment.

Preheat your oven to 350F/180C/Gas 4.

In a large bowl mix together the grated carrots, sugar, oil and eggs.

In a separate bowl combine the flour, cocoa powder, baking powder and salt. Now gradually whisk the wet ingredients into the dry.

Pour into the prepared baking tins.

Bake in the oven for 25-30 minutes.

Cool for ten minutes in the pan then turn out.

To make the frosting whisk the butter and sugar together until light and fluffy, then mix in the melted chocolate.

Fill the cake with frosting and decorate the top.

Chocolate Mocha Cookies
These are a nice crisp cookie that have a deep chocolatey taste but with a hint of fired up coffee to give you a boost.

230g/8.1 oz butter, softened
110g/3.9 oz caster sugar
230g/8.1 oz plain/all-purpose flour
60g/2.1 oz cornflour
60g/2.1 oz cocoa powder
10g/0.35 oz instant coffee powder

Preheat your oven to 350F/180C/Gas 4. Line two baking sheets with baking parchment.

Grind the coffee powder with a pestle and mortar or the back of a spoon so that it is a fine powder.

Whisk the butter and sugar in a bowl until light and fluffy.

In a separate bowl mix together the flour, cornflour, cocoa powder and ground coffee powder. Add the dry ingredients to the butter sugar mixture, stir to combine. It should come together to form a dough.

Wrap in cling film and pop in the fridge for half an hour.

Dust a worktop with flour and roll out your dough so that it is about ¼ thick (6mm). Cut circles out with a cookie cutter (about 2 ¼"). Place onto the prepared baking sheets. They won't spread much.

You should get about 30 cookies.

Chill for a further 15 minutes in the fridge.

Bake for 15-20 minutes.

Saffron Cupcakes
Saffron is an ancient spice that brings a really unique flavour, it has quite an earthy taste but with a fire behind it. Saffron also gives a bright yellow/orange colour to any food you use it in.

    1 tablespoon butter, softened
    1 tablespoon sugar
    180g/6.4oz plain/all-purpose flour
    200g/7 oz sugar

1 teaspoon baking powder
1/2 teaspoon bicarbonate soda
150ml/5 fl oz plus 2 tablespoons milk
1 teaspoon saffron threads
1 egg
1 teaspoon vanilla extract

Sugar syrup
118ml/4 fl oz cup water
150g/5.3 oz sugar
1 teaspoon vanilla extract

Icing
75g/2.6 oz icing/powdered sugar
Water
Few drops of food colouring (optional)

Preheat your oven to 350F/180C/Gas 4.

Mix together the flour, sugar, baking powder and bicarbonate soda.

In a small pan heat the two tablespoons milk with the saffron threads, bring to a simmer whilst stirring, then remove from the heat, allow to cool.

In a separate bowl mix 150ml of milk with the egg and one teaspoon of the vanilla extract. Add the cooled saffron milk and mmix.

Pour the wet ingredients into the flour mixture and whisk to combine.

Place 12 cupcake cases into a cupcake tin.

Pour the batter equally between the 12 cases.

Bake for 20 minutes.

Stir 150g sugar into the 118ml of water and pop into a small pan over a low heat. Simmer for ten minutes, stirring occasionally. Stir in one teaspoon of vanilla extract.

Poke holes evenly in the cupcakes with a skewer. Spoon the vanilla syrup over the top of each of the warm cupcakes. Allow to cool.

To make the icing mix the icing sugar with a few teaspoons of water, add a teaspoon at a time until you get the right consistency.

Add in a few drops of food colouring if you would like.

Spoon the icing over the cupcakes and allow to set.

Key Lime Cupcakes (vegan option)
A lovely soft sponge cake topped with a very zingy lime frosting that makes your eyes water.

275g/9.7 oz plain/all-purpose flour
225g/8 oz sugar
1 teaspoon bicarbonate soda
Pinch salt
Juice of 1 lime
Milk (can be plant based) approx. 225ml/8 fl oz
Zest from 2 limes
75g/2.6 oz vegetable oil
1 tablespoon cider vinegar
1 teaspoon vanilla extract
A few drops green food colouring

Frosting
375g/13.2 oz icing/powdered sugar
56g/2 oz butter (can be vegan)
3 tablespoons lime juice
A few drops green food colouring

Preheat your oven to 350F/180C/Gas 4.

Pop the flour, sugar, bicarbonate soda and salt into a large bowl.

In a measuring jug add the juice of one lime. Now top up with milk to the 225ml/8 fl oz line. It will curdle, this is supposed to happen.

Pour the milk into the dry ingredients. Add the lime zest, oil, vinegar, vanilla extract and a few drops of food colouring.

Whisk until you have a smooth batter.

Line a cupcake tray with 12 cake liners and divide the batter equally between them.

Bake for 25 minutes.

Remove from the oven and cool.

To make the frosting whisk the butter and icing sugar until thick and smooth. Then whisk in the lime juice and food colouring. Whisk until the colour is even.

If the frosting is too runny add a little more icing sugar. If the icing is too stiff add a little more lime juice.

Pipe the frosting onto each cupcake.

Exercise
Think about the elements as you cook your dinner or bake a cake. Connect with the energy of the ingredients.

Crystals

Each crystal will have an association with one of the elements, sometimes more than one.

The basic fact is that crystals are taken from Mother Earth and some of the mining practices can be extremely harsh to the environment. Only you can make the decision about where you source your crystals from. There are some very good eco-friendly crystal providers, it may just take a bit of research on your part. A lot of crystal suppliers are now stating their sources which is very helpful.

If you want to connect with the element of fire or use a fire crystal in your spell working, then these are some suggestions for crystals to use:

Agate magical properties (banded/brown/black)
Perception, wisdom, balance, spirituality, goodwill, peace, memory, concentration, stamina, truth, clarity, honesty, courage, protection, calming, sleep, dreams, strength, longevity, nature, love, anti-stress, energy

Energy: Projective
Element: Fire
Planet: Mercury

Amber magical properties:
Manifesting, energy, beauty, sun magic, power, wishes, intellect, clarity, wisdom, balance, purification, protection, psychic abilities, healing, calm, patience, love, sensuality, good luck, marriage, abundance, success, vitality, joy, sexuality, cleansing, stress, harmony, creativity

Energy: Projective

Element: Fire, Spirit
Planet: Sun

Bloodstone magical properties:
Organisation, adaptability, anxiety, clarity, concentration, renewal, energy, self-confidence, connection, calm, protection, breaking barriers, selfishness, mysticism, insight, spirituality, truth, intuition, creativity, guidance, strength, healing, victory, wealth, money, power, invisibility, deception, negative energy, divine connection, past life, dreams

Energy: Projective
Element: Fire, Earth
Planet: Mars

Carnelian magical properties
Grounding, protection, calm, concentration, confidence, self-worth, success, courage, creativity, negative energy, direction, control, organisation, opportunity, planning, psychic protection, jealousy, hate, harmony, depression, doubt, patience, stability, vitality, motivation, stamina, passion, truth, love, faith, honesty, trust, luck, abundance

Energy: Projective
Element: Fire
Planet: Sun

Citrine magical properties:
Happiness, joy, sun magic, negative energy, optimism, abundance, depression, stress, success, wealth, healing, intuition, creativity, confidence, changes, self-esteem, protection, psychic powers, fears, clarity, stamina, nightmares

Energy: Projective
Element: Fire
Planet: Sun, Jupiter

Garnet magical properties
Organisation, warrior spirit, protection, love, commitment, passion, sexuality, sensuality, attraction, depression, spiritual healing, success, self-confidence, energy, inspiration, perception, strength, survival, fear, courage, clarity, challenges, past life work, truth, compassion, deflecting negative energy, gossip, ambition, motivation, goals, purification, cleansing, balance, inner strength, self-empowerment, creativity, confidence, meditation, spirit work, nightmares, journeying, abundance, support

Energy: Projective
Element: Fire
Planet: Mars

Gold magical properties
Prosperity, action, power, healing, renewal, self-esteem, wealth, all round sunshine energy, wisdom, learning, potential, self-confidence, self-worth, calm, negative energy, transformation, spirituality, nature, happiness, energy, stress, the divine, sun magic, ritual, illumination, understanding

Energy: Projective
Element: Fire
Planet: Sun

Goldstone magical properties
Ambition, luck, goals, determination, persistence, achievements, success, calm, emotions, energy, enthusiastic, confidence, self-belief, inner self, personal development, possibilities, courage, direction, clarity, uplifting, optimism, protection, deflects negative energy, knowledge, perception, manifestation, creativity, faith, energy flow, spirituality, abundance, wealth, grounding, perspective, ambition, drive, ingenuity, money, generosity, willpower, goals, emotions, divination (see also copper for additional magical properties)

Energy: Receptive/Projective
Element: Fire, Earth
Planet: Jupiter, Venus

Hematite magical properties
Grounding, money, decisions, manifestation, finances, healing, focus, clarity, stability, protection, balance, divination, problem solving, emotions, self-esteem, productivity, doubt, anxiety, communication, strength

Energy: Projective
Element: Fire, Earth
Planet: Saturn

Jasper (red/brick) magical properties
Guardian, protective, defensive magic, deflecting negative energy, health, healing, beauty, transformation, balance, stability

Energy: Projective
Element: Fire
Planet: Mars

Jasper (black) magical properties
Personal space, protection, ritual, invisibility

Energy: Projective
Element: Fire
Planet: Uranus

Larimar magical properties
Peace, clarity, healing, inspiration, spirituality, understanding, calming, soothing, uplifting, emotions, fears, depression, patience, creativity, love, communication, friendship, guidance, happiness, decisions, relaxation, meditation, wisdom, divine, harmony

Energy: Receptive
Element: Water/Fire/Spirit
Planet: Neptune

Obsidian (black) magical properties
Truth, healing, clarity, illusions, breaking barriers, integrity, grounding, centring, strength, courage, protection, cleansing, meditation, stress, calming, relaxation, depression, anxiety, wealth, luck, focus, emotions, power, determination, success, patience, perseverance, releasing, spirit work, spirituality, challenges, past life work, divination

Energy:	Projective
Element:	Fire, Earth, Water
Planet:	Saturn, Jupiter

Pyrite magical properties
Releasing, breaking patterns, clarity, protection, support, decisions, growth, success, inspiration, grounding, vitality, learning, perception, memory, wisdom, psychic abilities, healing, cleansing, prosperity, wealth, abundance, luck, strength, motivation, manifestation, finances, energy, sun magic, power, focus, perseverance, confidence, divination, communication, self-confidence, meditation

Energy:	Projective
Element:	Fire
Planet:	Mars, Sun

Quartz (clear) magical properties
Purification, cleansing, healing, calming, emotions, strength, support, spirituality, energy, balance, psychic abilities, motivation, uplifting, decisions, anxiety, divine connection, amplifying, focus, meditation, manifestation, channelling, protection, negative energy, clarity, wisdom, concentration, learning, spirit work, communication, astral travel, divination, dreams, harmony

Energy:	Projective, Receptive
Element:	Fire, Water
Planet:	Sun, Moon

Rhodochrosite magical properties
Power, potential, strength, confidence, healing, new beginnings, breaking barriers, releasing, joy, happiness, creativity, determination, manifestation, prosperity, abundance, love, emotions, peace, renewal, connection, balance, spirituality, harmony, energy

Energy:	Projective
Element:	Fire
Planet:	Mars, Jupiter

Rhodonite magical properties
Protection, renewal, emotions, strength, soothing, clarity, happiness, love, balance, harmony, decisions, confidence, spirituality, peace, energy, passion, optimism, changes, vitality, anxiety, travel, psychic abilities, self-confidence, trust, calming, relaxation, patience, determination, releasing, stress, negative energy

Energy:	Projective
Element:	Fire
Planet:	Mars, Venus

Serpentine magical properties
Meditation, peace, clarity, nature, fairy magic, emotions, calming, protection, negative energy, love, prosperity, manifestation, psychic protection, success, cleansing

Energy:	Projective
Element:	Fire
Planet:	Saturn

Sunstone magical properties
Sun magic, power, decisions, leadership, strength, happiness, inspiration, love, luck, stability, clarity, energy, stress, depression, emotions, optimism, perseverance, intuition, fears, self-esteem, self-confidence, healing, balance, harmony,

abundance, prosperity, opportunities, peace, protection

Energy: Projective
Element: Fire
Planet: Sun

Tiger's Eye magical properties
Amplification, balance, harmony, releasing, fears, anxiety, courage, strength, self-confidence, focus, creativity, optimism, self-worth, protection, psychic abilities, healing, wealth, money, opportunity, abundance, prosperity, luck, success, commitment, determination, support, clarity, vitality, motivation, grounding, patience

Energy: Projective
Element: Fire, Earth
Planet: Sun

Tourmaline (watermelon/red) magical properties
Calming, harmony, balance, insight, spirituality, protection, negative energy, transformation, courage, grounding, fears, creativity, understanding, power, motivation, commitment, patience, stability, releasing, emotions, anxiety, strength, happiness, protection, relaxation, friendship, astral travel

Energy: Projective
Element: Fire
Planet: Venus, Mars

Unakite magical properties
Love, happiness, growth, wealth, success, harmony, decisions, support, balance, emotions, stability, confidence, strength, anxiety, nature, courage, transformation, releasing, spirituality

Energy: Receptive
Element: Fire, Water
Planet: Mars, Venus, Pluto

Exercise

Keep a record of your crystals and any experiences you have with them. Are there any that you found particularly linked to the element of fire?

Fire Animals

I love working with animal spirit guides. Each animal has a very unique energy and they can help and guide you, but also lend their characteristics to your spell work. Each animal has an element that they are associated with, it might be with their build, look, habits or where they live. Here are some suggestions for fire element animals:

Bee – Keywords: Prosperity, good fortune, communication, gossip, reincarnation, goals, celebration, community, achieving your dreams, productivity, co-operation and focus.

Cat – Keywords: Independence, healing, curiosity, mystery, psychic abilities, elegance, intuition, mystery, wisdom, understanding and balance.

Coyote – Keywords: Intelligence, stealth, trust, fun, shape shifting, balance, cunning, wisdom, mistakes, reflection, karma, connections, protection, nurturing, adapting, negotiations.

Dragon – Keywords: Strength, courage, energy – other meanings are specific to the type of dragon.

Fox – Keywords: Cunning, stealth, courage, observation, persistence, wisdom, magic, shape shifting and invisibility.

Hawk – Keywords: Messages, Underworld, communication, magic, observation, vigilance, intuition, perspective, past lives, overcoming problems, opportunities, courage, defence, creativity, truth, decisions.

Horse – Keywords: Friendship, faithfulness, freedom, endurance, power, energy, travel, loyalty, overcoming obstacles, fertility and strength.

Ladybird/bug – Keywords: Trust, faith, wishes, luck, protection, happiness, intuition, defence, past lives, cycle of life and enlightenment.

Lion – Keywords: Sun magic, goddess magic, hunt, community, sharing, protection, strength, courage, co-operation, maternity, vengeance, being heard, relaxation, family and stress release.

Lizard – Keywords: Facing your fears, guidance, balance, re-birth, wisdom, good fortune and the cycle of life.

Panther/Leopard – Keywords: Malice, fierceness, bravery, courage, grace, pacing yourself, pressure, timeframes, life, death and rebirth.

Phoenix – Keywords: Death and rebirth, renewal, healing, passion, strength, creativity and growth.

Porcupine – Keywords: Determination, trust, power, fun, imagination, protection, defence, patience, vulnerability, sensitivity, solidarity.

Scorpion – Keywords: Transition, sex, control, solitary, passion, protection, defence and vulnerability.

Shark – Keywords: Unpredictable, courage, protection, confidence, water magic, visions, psychic work, activity, hunter, survival, adaptability, independence, emotions and balance.

Snake – Keywords: Transformation, fertility, astral travel, creativity, sexuality, power, spirituality and healing, wisdom.

Squirrel – Keywords: Removing obstacles, solving problems, resourcefulness, preparing, planning ahead, balance, knowing when to rest, playful, action, communication and trust.

Tiger – Keywords: Emotions, intuition, spontaneity, power, personal strength, courage, overcoming obstacles, vitality, healing and aggression.

Exercise

Keep an eye out for any animals that you see during your day. Not just outside, but also when reading a book, watching TV or adverts in magazines or on billboards. Take note of any animal images you might also see on fabrics, cushions or clothing. If you keep seeing the same one, it may have meaning for you.

Fire Animal meditation

This meditation will help you meet a fire animal spirit guide. It may be just a message for you, it might be with you for longer, talk to it and ask. Find a comfortable place where you won't be disturbed. Take a few deep breaths, in and out...

As your world around you dissipates you find yourself standing at a crossroads. The sky above you is clear blue and the sun is shining high in the sky.

Beneath your feet the ground is a dry dusty dirt track.

The road in front of you appears to lead to high rocky mountains.

To your right the road leads to a sandy shore line.

Behind you the road takes you to a tropical forest.

And to your left a gate beckons with a beautiful garden behind it.

Which road will you take?

Trust your intuition and head down the road that most draws you in.

As you enter the destination that your choice took you to. Look around you.

What is above you? What is beneath your feet? What is the scenery like, the landscape and the vegetation?

Find a spot that looks comfortable and sit down.

Now ask out loud for your fire element animal guide to meet you.

Wait, listen and watch.

It might be a fleeting glance at first. You may need to come back a few times to gain their confidence.

They may just pitch up right in front of you.

Some will have a message and deliver it to you right now. Others may be with you for longer and have insight to share with you over time.

Look, listen, learn.

Be open to whatever comes to you.

When it makes contact, ask questions...

And when you are ready, thank the creature and head back the way you came.

Know that you can visit here again and take a different path if you wish.

When you are ready slowly and gently come back to the here and now. Open your eyes and wriggle your fingers and toes.

If you met an animal that is going to be with you for a while it would be worth setting up a small altar to them if you are able to. Print an image from the internet of the creature or find a small ornament that represents them. Leave an offering on the altar to thank them for their attention.

Exercise
Write down your fire animal experience, if you met a particular animal do some research on it.

Dragon Magic

Dragon magic is an ancient and fascinating subject and one that covers so much that we couldn't possibly fit it all in this book, but, hopefully, what I have tried to do here is cover the basics and maybe whet your appetite just a little.

There are different views of what dragons are and of what they represent. They are sometimes viewed as mythological entities which represent a set of principles. Dragons can be associated with each of the elements, types of landscape or areas of the country. However, overall, I do believe dragons embody the element of fire, which is why they are here in this book.

A Dragon viewed as a winged serpent could be a symbol of the earth and the underworld. The wings as a symbol of the heavens. The winged serpent brings together these two principles – as above, so below. The Chinese dragon is a symbol of Tao, that which is beyond all terms and all polarities but also the force behind all (Yin and Yang).

The Dragon represents the unknown, the hidden energy in humans and in nature. The word dragon comes from the Greek verb 'derkein' which means 'to see'. The Dragon is the principle of clear seeing: the ability to see things in a new light as they really are, beyond all illusions.

You might be familiar with the idea of a dragon hording his treasure; it is that treasure that symbolises the wisdom it keeps. For us to find the knowledge it guards we must look for it within ourselves and venture into the mysteries to find the answers. If you have ever practiced yoga you will know the dragon as the Kundalini, the force that is hidden inside us. We all have it within us to awaken the forces within the dragon.

The world of Dragon has so many different breeds, types, colours, sizes and shapes. Some you may be more familiar with than others – the Chinese or the Welsh Dragon for instance, others such as the Worm of Wyrd maybe new to you. But no matter what they look like, they all hold incredible power.

A dragon can be a strong, useful and wise totem or guardian and we can also tap into dragon energy to use within our rituals and our magic. Dragons are a primeval force, they are physical and spiritual, they bring with them the full force and power of the elements. They are also very wise and intelligent. If you are familiar with energy work and maybe even sensing energy fields, if you pick up the feeling of a large energy field around you then chances are it may be a dragon.

Whether dragons did used to roam the earth I don't know, I like to think so. But now they exist in the astral and spiritual plane. Dragon Energy is one of the most powerful energies I know of and when blended together via the four main elements, creates the etheric dragon… a super power.

Dragon energy is linear, so be careful what you ask for. You will receive it in the most direct way possible. Be very specific about your intentions, integrity and intelligence. Dragons do not necessarily use human logic, if you offer them a problem, they will find a solution, but it will be a straight forward one, removing anything in its path to solve it. Dragon energy is very good at removing dark energy, it is good for clearing negative energy but make sure you also ask for positive energy to be left in its place. Dragon magic works quickly and can sometimes have unexpected results.

As Witches usually have an element we favour to work with, so do dragons. Not everyone believes that we have 'elemental dragons' as such, they aren't necessarily made up from one particular element, just that they work best with one element, although you will also find a few that work well with all the elements, these are particularly powerful.

Whilst I don't want to put you off working with dragons, I would ask you to remember that these are very old and very wise creatures they also have a tendency to get bored easily and are impatient! (A lot like myself.) So always treat them with the respect that you would a wise elder. What I can tell you is that working with dragon energy can be very beneficial and a wonderful experience. Dragons also have so much to teach us, all that ancient wisdom waiting to be shared with us not to mention all their powerful energy and support that they can provide us with.

And a word about the chaos dragon, usually dark purple in colour and really a bit of a mischief maker. Just keep an eye on him and you will be fine, he is however extremely useful to call upon when you need to 'undo' a spell.

Dragon Lines

You will all have probably heard the term 'ley lines' before, magnetic fields of energy that form lines crossing and intersecting over the earth.

Centuries ago, the Chinese called ley lines 'Dragon Lines'. When the Dragon Lines cross each other their energy spirals and becomes a vortex. If several lines cross at a certain point (a node) it can produce a huge vortex of energy. Avebury in the UK has 12 lines that meet and go down into the Earth; this is where the stones are placed.

Dragon Healing

Dragon energy is very useful for healing; you can channel it when using crystal healing or in hands on healing but there is also a form of Reiki that combines dragon energy too for the purpose of healing.

In Ritual

You can call upon dragons in your quarter calls, as you would call in the elements.

Dragon Guide/Guardian

Having a dragon spirit animal guide is very special; they are incredibly powerful and wise. If Dragon appears as your guide it usually means you need one or some of their qualities such as strength or courage, they also bring the message of balance and ask us to use our psychic abilities to see the world as magical.

Once Dragon has come to you, I do encourage you to connect with it on a regular basis, make a connection and keep it, a dragon totem is very useful not only as a powerful guardian but also as a guide – keep it happy!

There are many ways to strengthen your bond with your Dragon. Here are a few suggestions:

- Meditate to converse with your Dragon.
- Collect dragon images – statues, pendants or pictures.
- Read everything you can on Dragons, this will not only strengthen your connection but expand your knowledge too.

Dragon possesses the following energies:
Leadership, magical prowess, vitality, mastery, insight, divine illumination, protection from outside evil forces from all directions, grounded energy, fulfilment of potential, inspiration, longevity, personal happiness, greatly increased riches, infinite wisdom, luminous beauty, majesty, indomitable spirit and strength, invisibility, power of transformation and metaphysical knowledge.

Dragon Types
These are just a few descriptions of some of the many dragon types:

- Chinese dragons (Chinese: lóng or "lung") These dragons are typically portrayed as long, scaled, serpentine creatures with four legs. Chinese dragons traditionally symbolize potent and auspicious powers, particularly control over water, rainfall, and floods. In yin and yang terminology, a dragon is yang (male) and complements a yin (female) fenghuang "Chinese phoenix".

- Japanese dragon myths amalgamate native legends with imported stories about dragons from China, Korea and India. Like these other Asian dragons, most Japanese ones are water deities associated with rainfall and bodies of water, and are typically depicted as large, wingless, serpentine creatures with clawed feet.

- European dragons are often referred to as a Wyrm or Wurm. This terminology can be confusing as wyrms are also described as a type of dragon with a long slender body, often able to breathe fire, with either none or four limbs but usually without wings. Derives from the Old Germanic 'Gewurm'.

- In European folklore, a dragon is a serpentine legendary creature. The Latin word 'draco', as in constellation Draco, comes directly from Greek. The word for dragon in Germanic mythology and its descendants is worm (Old English: wyrm, Old High German: wurm, Old Norse: ormr), meaning snake or serpent. In Old English 'wyrm' means 'serpent', draca means 'dragon'.

- Finnish lohikäärme means directly 'salmon-snake', but the word lohi- was originally louhi- meaning crags or rocks, a 'mountain snake'. Though a winged creature, the dragon is generally to be found in its underground lair, a cave.

- In Western folklore, dragons are usually portrayed as evil, with the exceptions mainly appearing in modern fiction. In the modern period the dragon is typically depicted as a huge fire-breathing, scaly and horned dinosaur-like creature, with leathery wings, with four legs and a long muscular tail. It is sometimes shown with feathered wings, crests, fiery manes, ivory spikes running down its spine and various exotic colorations.

Celtic Tradition

In Celtic mythology the dragon was considered as a benevolent dweller of caves, lakes and the inner earth. In ancient times, it was a symbol of wealth and associated with the power of the elements, but also of the treasure of the subconscious mind. Dragons often appeared in many varieties: as a water serpent or worm-shaped beast, as well as the more well-known winged depiction. The dragon represented the supernatural forces that guarded the great secrets and treasures of the universe.

The Fire Dragon is a symbol of transmutation, energy and mastery, if you are working with this dragon you will find enthusiasm, courage and vitality. Your inner fire will be fuelled. You will be helped to overcome obstacles. You will be given the qualities of leadership and mastery. The fire dragon can also be a strong protector. The name Pendragon is most often linked with the great King Arthur. The name Pendragon however did not start with King Arthur, but with his father Uther. He saw an image of a fire-breathing dragon in the sky. Uther went to the Druid Merlin to decipher the meaning of the fire dragon he had seen. Merlin told him that the fire dragon was a symbol of his ill brother's pending death, and his own future kinghood. 'Pendragon', translates as 'Head of the Dragon'. Uther had two dragon statues constructed, one of which became his insignia. King Arthur and later kings continued the Pendragon name and the dragon symbol became a heraldic emblem.

The Air Dragon brings insight, inspiration and vitality. This dragon must be handled with the greatest of respect (as they all should). With this dragon you may receive illumination in intellect and psyche. Insight and clarity will be given for all problems. As always – trust your intuition.

Air dragons have been sighted throughout different regions of the United Kingdom. Some believe that the sightings were comets passing close to the earth. Stories of dragons may have also arisen from thieves wanting to keep the locals away from their stolen treasure. Snowdonia, Wales is home to the ancient city of Emrys, also known as, Dinas Affaron to the locals, which translates as 'City of the Higher Powers'. In this city lived the dragons of Beli. Beli Mawr is often depicted riding a horse drawn chariot across the sky. He is also connected to Dragon Hill, below the Uffington Horse.

Perhaps the horse leading Beli Mawr across the sky was not meant to be a horse but a dragon instead? Taliesin the Welsh bard described one of Beli's dragons in a poem called 'Protection of the Honey Isle'. There are stories of the Goddess Cerridwen riding across the skies with her chariot drawn by flying dragons.

The Earth Dragon brings potential, power and riches. You will be shown your potential and your riches – what you are capable of. With the earth dragon's assistance, you may discover the beauty and power that lies within you, within us all. The earth dragon resides deep within the Earth and can aid you in grounding scattered energies. In England the large chalk figure of the Uffington Horse, located in Oxfordshire has long been thought to represent a dragon instead of a horse. The story suggest that St. George once slew a dragon, on a nearby hill called Dragon Hill, and the symbol is a portrait of the dragon. The dragon's blood poisoned the ground where he was defeated and to this day grass does not grow in this spot. Although there is still controversy surrounding the symbol, the dragon and the horse share the same symbol of earth energy and with the power of the land.

The Water Dragon brings connection, depth and passion. The water dragon brings memories and wishes, hidden mysteries are opened up to you. By diving into past experiences, a sense of peace and balance can be found. The water dragon will give you the courage and compassion in this challenge.

The water dragon began its life as a worm, a large snake or eel-like creature, sometimes with horns, that lived in the wells, lochs, or the sea. At some stage the worm grew small wings and two feet and became known as the Wyvern. The worm later became a Dragon with four feet, large ribbed wings, and a barbed tail. These dragons were said to sometimes leave the water and terrorize the hills and country they settled in. The ones that remained in the water were depicted as sea monsters, the most famous living in Loch Ness.

Dragon Meditation:
Make yourself comfortable in a place where you won't be disturbed. Close your eyes and focus on your breathing.

Your world around you dissipates and you find yourself in a clearing, in the distance you can see mountains and what looks like a volcano top with smoke creeping out of its crater. Behind you is a large dense forest and to one side you turn to see a large lake.

Look up towards the sky and see the storm clouds rolling in from over the mountain tops, although the sun is still trying to break through and long shafts of light beam down on the surface of the lake making it glint and sparkle.

You realise you are not alone, flying high above you are shapes that look like large birds, on a second look you realise they are dragons, dark shapes weaving in and out of the clouds.

Then you hear crashing sounds coming from the forest and realise that behind the trees large dragons are moving around. But you don't feel afraid.

Splashing from the lake draws your attention and you notice that some of the glints in the water are actually dragons swimming and splashing, breaking the surface of the water.

A loud roaring sound draws your attention to the mountain tops and you see that diving in and out of the volcano crater are dragons,

breathing long streams of flame as they dive.
Then on the shoreline of the lake you realise what you thought were
sandy rocks are actually large desert dragons sunning themselves.
Stand for a moment and draw on the powers of all these different
dragons, reach out with your mind and see if one of them makes a
connection with you.
If one does, ask it to join you where you are standing. Wait until it
stands beside you then ask for permission to ask it some questions.
If it agrees then ask what you want to know.
Once you are finished, thank the dragon for its presence, guidance
and wisdom and bid it farewell. It may tell you that it is your
dragon guardian now and you can call upon it any time, it may not.
Know that you can always come back to the land of dragons for
guidance.

Slowly bring your focus back to the present, shake your arms and legs and open your eyes.

Exercise
Do the dragon meditation and journal your experience. If you met a dragon in the meditation do some research on its type, if you didn't meet one pick a dragon type that attracts you and make a note of what its characteristics are, what qualities it has.

Fire deities
Each deity is usually associated with one of the elements more than the others. Please do your research first. I would never recommend calling upon a god without knowing a proper amount of information about them first. Learn about their culture, myths and stories before you ask for their help. Here are some suggestions for deities that correspond with the element of fire, the list is only a start, there are a lot more. I have only given brief descriptions, if any of them sing out to you, I encourage you to research and investigate further.

Agni – Hindu god of fire. He is the fire of the sun, lightening and the hearth of the home and the sacrificial hearth. He is a messenger between humans and the divine, being the speaker for the gods. He brings protection for humankind and safety for the home. He is believed to have two faces, one is beneficent and the other malignant. His hair stands out on end like flames, he has three legs and seven arms. Often seen with three or seven tongues and accompanied by a ram. He is quite a sight to behold. He guards the south east direction. Call on Agni for all kinds of fire magic, communication, home, solar magic, protection and sacrifice (of the mental, emotion kind not animals or humans!).

Amaterasu – Shinto sun goddess who rules Takama no Hara (the High Celestial Plain). Her full name Amaterasu Ōmikami means 'the great divinity illuminating heaven'. She was born from her father, Izanagi's left eye. She is manifested in a mirror that is one of the three Imperial Treasures of Japan, it can be found in her main place of worship, the Grand Shrine of Ise in Japan. Call upon her for solar magic, mirror magic, creativity, inspiration, divine connection.

Astarte – Goddess from the ancient Middle East. She is a goddess of war, sex, love and fertility. Depicted quite often naked wearing nothing more than a set of bull horns on her head she is most definitely full of warrior power. I say she, but her body is often seen as androgynous. She rules over horses and many images of her show her on horseback or with horses in the scene. Some sources believe her father to be the sun god Ra, others suggest Ptah, the god of craftsmen. Call upon Astarte for sex magic, fertility, power, love, sexuality, strength.

Bast/Bastet – Egyptian goddess of the home, domesticity, female energy, fertility, childbirth and cats. She is the original 'mad cat lady'. She brings protection to the home but also looks out for women and children, for their safety, health and well-being. Daughter of the sun god Ra she brings clarity and transformation. Images show her originally in the form of a lioness but later with the head of a cat. Call upon her for protection, female energy, fertility, childbirth, domestic matters, the home, clarity, transformation.

Belenus – One of the most widely recognised Celtic pagan gods His name translates as 'bright or brilliant one'. His festival is thought to be held at Beltane. At this time the cattle were led between bonfires to purify them and bring good luck for the coming season. There is a debate as to whether Belenus was worshipped as a sun god I include him here because that's how I work with him, as do a lot of other pagans. Although some artifacts have been found showing what is believed to be Belenus with a halo of light around his head. If it fits…go with it. Call upon him for healing, solar magic, purification, fire magic, protection.

Brigit/Brighid/Brigid – An Irish deity, daughter of Dagda. She was hijacked by Christianity at some point and made into a Saint. Often associated with the sabbat of Imbolc. She has a sacred fire that burns continuously in Kildare, Ireland. Call upon her for creativity, crafts, divination, fire magic, fertility, growth, healing.

Hephaestus/Hephaistos – Greek god of fire. Hephaestus is patron to black smiths and all craftsmen. He made the famous winged helmet and sandals for the god Hermes and a suit of armour for Achilles (pity he didn't make him some boots as well…). He had mad creative skills, something like Q from the Bond films. He is associated with all elements of fire including volcanoes. Call upon him for crafting, inspiration, fire magic, magical tools, determination.

Hestia – Greek goddess of the hearth and home. She embodied the hearth and home and sacrifices in all temples were received by Hestia. She also received the first and last libation offerings at feasts. Call upon her for home, stability, sacrifice, family, union, communication, disputes, hospitality, protection, devotion, manifestation.

Freyr – Norse fertility god he also covers the sun, rain, harvests and all agriculture. He is a god of the land. His side kick is a trusty wild boar. Although his main focus is fertility of all kinds, he also covers battle and warrior energy. Call upon him for sun magic, weather magic, manifesting, growth, courage.

Kali – Hindu goddess of death, time and feminine energy. With her blue skin, tongue sticking out and carrying severed heads she is quite a sight to see. Her name translates as 'she who is black or she who is death'. She can be a caring mother figure but also sexuality and violence come under her remit. Call upon her for death & rebirth, feminine energy, creativity, fertility, sexuality, power, time, cycles, cleansing, change.

Lugh – Celtic god of sun and light. Originally seen as a deity, it seems later on he was noted as a great warrior and Irish hero. He kills Balor in battle using a magic spear and sling, this kicks off 40 years of peace and good fortune for the country. Call upon him for solar magic, creativity, inspiration, crafts, divination, the arts.

Mars – Roman god of war. His Greek counterpart is Ares. He was a protector of Rome and the way of life. The month of March bears his name. Call upon Mars for protection, passion, destruction, courage.

Pele – Hawaiian goddess of volcanoes, she is said to have re-created the islands with the power of volcanoes. She looks after her people and her lands. Call upon her for creativity, change, unity, traditions, protection, transformation.

Di Penates/Penates – Roman gods of the household. A group of gods that took care of each home and those within. Houses had a shrine that contained images of the gods to which offerings of food were made. Not particularly a group you would call upon for working magic, but perhaps something to bear in mind when working with the home and household protection.

Prometheus – Greek god, one of the Titans. He is a god of fire and a trickster. His name translates as 'forethinker'. The fire connection comes from his skills as a craftsman. Zeus is said to have taken fire and hidden it from us mortals, Prometheus was the one that stole it and returned it to us. Call upon him for challenges, changes, creativity, inspiration, intellect, cunning, fire magic.

Ra – Perhaps one of the most recognised sun gods, Ra is the sun and creator god from ancient Egypt. During the day he travels across the sky and by night he traverses the underworld. The name 'Ra' literally means 'sun'. You will find his name in various forms that show different aspects such as Amun Re. Call upon him for sun magic, creativity, courage, power, growth.

Sulis – a goddess from ancient Britain, her base of operations is Bath, Somerset in the UK at the source of the natural springs. Once the Romans arrived, they took her over and merged her with their own goddess, Minerva. She is a sun goddess of healing and divination. Call upon her for solar magic, healing, water magic, divination.

Vesta – Roman goddess of the hearth and home, her Greek

counterpart is Hestia. First born of the Titans. The hearth played an important role in Roman households as it did and still does in many homes across the glove. It provided heat, cooking of food and enabled them to heat water. Call upon her for home, fire magic, kitchen magic, love, fertility, peace.

Vulcan – Roman god of fire, volcanoes and relegation. He not only created and worked with fire but was also called upon to protect against fires. He was a great craftsman, which it seems is something a lot of these fiery gods have in common. Apparently, he was quite ugly to look at. Call upon him for fire magic, transformation, creativity, crafting, inspiration.

Wayland/Weland – an Anglo Saxon god of smithcraft. Some stories suggest he was a lord to the elves. It is said that once captured he killed the two sons of his captor and made drinking bowls from their skulls. In Norse mythology you will find him equated with Volund. Call upon him for crafting, creativity, revenge, inspiration.

Fire deity meditation
If you are interested in working with a fire deity you can pick one from the list above and do some research on them. If you prefer, I find that meditation is an excellent way to discover new deities.

Find a comfortable place where you won't be disturbed. Take a few deep breaths, in and out...

> *As your world around you dissipates you find yourself standing in the centre of a stone courtyard. The sky above you is bright clear blue and the sun is right above your head.*
> *The stone beneath your feet is a pale golden colour, large slabs are set side by side to create a floor.*
> *You are surrounded by enormous stone pillars, created from the*

same material as the floor.

There is no roof, the sun shines down upon you and the architecture around you.

At one end there appears to be a long altar set into the wall, in the centre of which is a fire, burning brightly.

Make your way to the altar and stand in front of the fire.

The altar is laid out with dishes full of different dried herbs and spices, slips of parchment paper and quills with bottles of coloured ink.

Further along there is a dish with incense on top of charcoal, the smoke rising, snaking up into the air and filling it with a heady spicy scent.

As you stand quietly watching the flames and the incense smoke you hear someone approach.

A figure enters the courtyard...

What do they look like? How are they dressed?

They approach you and introduce themselves.

They ask if there is anything they can help you with, and you find yourself answering them honestly and comfortably.

They listen...

Then you are directed to write a petition on the parchment from the altar.

You select some paper and a quill and dip into one of the coloured inks, writing your petition...

Following their guidance, you fold the parchment and throw it into the fire, selecting a few herbs and spices from the various dishes to throw into the fire afterwards.

Then the figure gives you some advice and guidance...you listen carefully.

When they are finished you thank them for their counsel and you are given a gift...

What is it and what does it mean to you?

The figure hugs you and then turns and walks away.

Spend some time thinking about what advice you were given.

When you are ready slowly and gently come back to the here and now. Open your eyes and wriggle your fingers and toes.

Exercise

Once you have met a deity in meditation and they have given you their name (they don't always give their name at first, sometimes not ever). I would recommend doing some research on them. Find out all you can about their stories and myths, along with the country they are associated with and any traditions. It will give you more insight into why they came to you and also as a matter of respect. It is also a wise precaution, so that you know who you are working with.

Fire Ritual

We probably all have our own way of working rituals. I have given my suggestion here but go with what works for you. I have included quarter calls for all four elements because I like the balance and I think the elements support each other. However, you could just call upon the element of fire if you prefer. I have given a ritual template here, use the deity list within this book for your gods and goddesses and also spell work to include, or add your own. I suggest you work a ritual for only one intent at a time, don't mix them up, it could confuse the energy.

Calling the Quarters

When in ritual most pagans will 'call in the quarters'. What does that mean? Well, we invite the four elements to join us and add their energy and qualities to the ritual. Each element corresponding to the four compass points. Some traditions choose to call in the Watchtowers or Guardians of the Watchtowers. The Guardians refer to the raw elementals and the Watchtowers are the directions.

Circle casting

Cast a circle to keep the positive energy raised within and to protect you from any negative outside influences. If you have the space you can walk the circle clockwise (to bring in energy) and perhaps sprinkle a corresponding fire herb or flower if you wish. You could also set out the circle physically with candles. If your space is limited, you can turn on the spot and visualise the circle. Make sure you 'see' the circle. Not only go around you but also above and below. You should end up with a visualised sphere or bubble around you. As you cast the circle you might like to add a chant such as:

I cast this circle round about
To keep unwanted energy out
Bringing in the element of fire
I cast this circle, my magic to inspire
So mote it be!

Being a bit of a Star Trek fan, I tend to use the phrase 'make it so' rather than 'so mote it be'. You may prefer to use your own words.

Call in your quarters

Your options are to just turn and face each direction as you call them in. Or you might like to light a candle at each direction. You could use items such as lighting incense in the east, a candle in the south, a dish of water in the west and a dish of soil in the north. If space is lacking you could work with a shell for west, a pebble for earth, a feather for air and a match for south. As we are working with the element of fire specifically you may just want to place a candle in the south and no items at all at the other points.

I start my quarter calls in the north, it seems to be the obvious compass point choice to me. A lot of witches and pagans start in the north. Although druids tend to begin their rituals by saluting the sun as it rises in the east. Follow your intuition. From the start point I turn clockwise. Give a call for each quarter, something like:

Element of earth
I invite you this ritual to tend
From the direction of North
Stability and grounding your energy to lend
Hail and welcome!

Element of air
I invite you this ritual to tend
From the direction of East
Intellect and wisdom your energy to lend
Hail and welcome!

Element of fire
I invite you this ritual to tend
From the direction of South
Passion and power your energy to lend
Hail and welcome!

Element of water
I invite you this ritual to tend
From the direction of West
Emotions and intuition your energy to lend
Hail and welcome!

Deity

It is entirely up to you whether you call upon deity for ritual or not. If you do, please make sure you do your research first. Not only would it be impolite to call upon a god that you don't know anything about, it could lend entirely the wrong energy to your ritual. Think about working a ritual for love and calling upon a war god...messy doesn't even begin to describe it.

Obviously, this book is all about the element of fire so I have suggested a list of fire deities, but you may be drawn in another direction. Trust your intuition but definitely do your homework too. I usually call upon a god and a goddess when working ritual, for me it brings a balance. But you don't have to, if you prefer to just call a god or a goddess then go for it. You may just prefer to call upon Mother Earth instead. Call in your deity with something like this:

> *I call upon the goddess Sulis,*
> *Asking that you bring your gifts of healing, happiness and energy to me*
> *Hail and welcome*

Basically, you call them by name and then ask them to bring whatever energy you need, so for Sulis as she is a solar goddess of healing you would call upon her for those gifts.

If you were performing a ritual with the intent of transformation, you might call upon Pele with:

> *I call upon the goddess Pele*
> *Asking that you guide me through my journey of transformation*
> *Hail and welcome"*

If it is a boost of creativity you are after, then Brighid is your gal:

> *I call upon the goddess Brighid*
> *Asking that you bring me the gift of inspiration to kick start my creativity*
> *Hail and welcome*

Spell work

Any ritual is created with a purpose, an intent in mind. What do you want to work this ritual for? Whatever it might be, this is the point in the ritual when you work your spell or even just use a meditation. Check out the spells and meditations suggested within this book or work with your own.

To the feast and drink

Once your spell work or meditation is done it is time for the feast. This really has double purpose. One is to celebrate with food and drink. A bit of a blessing in the form of 'may you never thirst' and 'may you never hunger'. Some of the food and drink is often sprinkled onto the earth if you are outside as a thank you to the gods and nature. Feasting also helps you to ground during the ritual, after any energy work has been done. It doesn't matter what you use to eat and drink. At our Kitchen Witch rituals, we always have cake, because that's how we roll. Often, I make cake that corresponds to the intent of the ritual, using particular ingredients and flavours to add to the will of the event. But you can use bread, sweets, fruits or biscuits. Mead or wine is a traditional ritual drink, but anything goes. At our rituals we often theme it, so we might have flavoured waters or herbals teas and in the cold, we have even had hot chocolate.

Now you close it all down in reverse...

Deity

Don't forget your manners, deity need to be thanked for attending the proceedings. It doesn't need to be fancy, just a simple one or two lines.

I thank the god/goddess for lending your energy to the rite today. Hail and farewell.

It really is that easy. But of course, you can add more text if you prefer.

Quarters

Next is thanking the elements in turn for their energy. Work in reverse order to that which you used initially. I start in the North when inviting the elements in, so I would now start with thanking water and working backwords to earth (North). Again, it doesn't need to be fancy, just something along the lines of:

I thank the element of earth for being here today, hail and farewell.

But I have made longer suggestions below:

Element of water
From the direction of West
Thank you for the energy you lent
Hail and farewell!

Element of fire
From the direction of South
Thank you for the energy you lent
Hail and farewell!

Element of air
From the direction of East
Thank you for the energy you lent
Hail and farewell!

Element of earth
From the direction of North
Thank you for the energy you lent
Hail and farewell!

Circle

Now the circle must be uncast. Walk widdershins (anti clockwise) around the circle and visualise the globe that you created, dispersing into the wind or back down into the soil:

I uncast this circle now the magic is all done
With my thanks for protection it gave
This circle is now open, but never broken
So mote it be!

Don't forget to give an offering to the earth if you didn't do so during the feasting. Dispose of any leftover spell working items and/or candles. Always leave the area clean and free from litter once you depart.

Fire spells

The element of fire aligns itself to several different intents, here are some of my suggestions for fire related spells. Follow them as I have laid them out or use them as a starting point to adjust with your own personal tweaks.

Cord Cutting Ritual

This is good to work with if you need to cut ties with someone or a situation. Sometimes friendships or relationships come to an end and it isn't always pleasant. Or it could be that you are connected with a toxic person and you want to distance yourself from them. It can also be a situation or issue rather than a person.

You will need:

A piece of cord, black or white is good but make sure it is safe to
burn
A candle, again black or white
Candle holder
Photo of yourself and one of the other person or the place – if you

don't have this then use two slips of paper and a pencil to write your/their names
Lighter or matches
Essential oil blend – a fiery one or plain such as clove or black pepper
Crushed black peppercorns
Fireproof dish or cauldron

Dress the candle with your essential oil, apply the oil outwards from the centre of the candle to the outer top and from the centre downwards to the bottom, as you want to release the energy.

Roll the candle in the crushed peppercorns.

Take your photographs or write your name and the other persons/place on two slips of paper. Roll them up together into a scroll and tie it up with the string, binding it around.

Light the candle.

Take the scroll and light the end of the cord from the candle flame.

Allow it to catch light then drop the scroll into the fireproof dish and allow it to burn out.

As you do so add in some magical words, perhaps something like this:

With the power and strength of fire
Cut the cords and release with this pyre
Set me free, with this I am now done
Releasing me to go have fun

Now sit quietly watching the candle flame and visualise yourself stepping away from the person or situation, see the spiritual and emotional cords being burnt away from between you.

Take some time now to visualise yourself being happy and free.

Allow the candle to burn down.

Dispose of the ashes by throwing them to the wind or dumping them in the trash.

Crystal Strength Spell

This is a simple spell that draws on the power of the crystal and the strength of the midday sun to bring you a charm for strength.

What you will need:

A crystal, carnelian is perfect for this

Take your crystal and set it on a window sill or outside in a safe place under the midday sun, when it is at its height and full strength.

Allow the crystal to soak up the solar energy for a short while, half an hour should do.

Take the crystal in your hand and hold it up to the sun (please don't look directly at the sun). Ask for solar energy to fill the crystal and bring you inner strength.

When you feel it is full, take the crystal and carry it with you.

If you feel the need for a boost of strength take hold of the crystal and draw upon that energy.

This can obviously be recharged easily if needed.

Banishing Spell

This is very easy to work with and can be used to remove unwanted people from your life or negative energy. Do remember when you banish something it leaves an empty void, nothing loves a void more than negative energy. Make sure you fill that space with positive energy instead.

You will need:

A black candle
Candle holder
Lighter or matches

Slip of paper
Pencil or pen
Fireproof dish or cauldron

Light the candle.

Write the name of the person or the issue, bad habit or situation you want removed from your life onto the slip of paper.

Now write your name over the top of theirs (or the issue), turn the paper a quarter turn and write your name over it again, turn a quarter turn again and write your name over the top. In total you want to write your name three times over theirs.

Now say something along the lines of:

I remove you, I release you, I discharge you from my life

Now carefully take the slip of paper and light it from the candle, drop it into the fireproof dish.

Allow the candle to burn out as you visualise that person or situation being banished from your life. Spend a few moments at the end visualising your life being filled with positive energy.

Dispose of the ashes in the trash.

Spell for transformation

Sometimes we need to bring about changes, it might be within ourselves and our behaviour patterns or it may be around us. You might want to transform your working or home life. To make a transformation successful requires action and that of releasing to allow it to unfold.

You will need:

A black candle
A white candle
A pale pink or pale yellow candle
Lighter or matches

A pen or pencil
Two pieces of paper
A pin or knife for carving
Essential oil blend such as cinnamon, frankincense or rosemary
Cauldron or fire proof dish

Take one sheet of paper and sit quietly with it in front of you. Pick up the pen and write 'let go of…'. Now just write, don't think about it too much, just let the words flow onto the paper. Even if it seems like the words are nonsense, write them down. It might be bad habits, a job you hate or a situation you are in.

When you feel you are finished take the second sheet of paper. Write at the top *'my goals'*. Think about what you would like to achieve and the goals you want to set. You can be as wild and free with these ideas as you want to. It might be changing how you eat or think. It could be a new career or way of life.

Now take the black candle and carve the word *'transformation'* into it. If the candle is small then just carve the letter *'T'* or a symbol that you feel represents transformation. Dress the candle with your essential oil. Place it in safe holder.

Take your white candle and carve your name or your initials into it, dress with oil and place in a safe holder.

With your pale yellow or pink candle, carve the words *'new beginning'* or if you are limited with space just carve the word *'new'*. Dress with oil and place in a safe holder.

Set the candles in line with the black one on your left, the coloured one in the centre and the white one on your right. Light all three candles.

Take the sheet of paper with the items you want to release, roll it up and light it from the black candle. Pop it into the cauldron to burn. As you watch the paper burning visualise letting go and release all of the things on the list.

Say a chant, something like:

Fiery transformation power of flame
Release and let go, without blame

Take the second sheet of paper with your goals, roll it up and light it from the white candle.

Pop it into the cauldron to burn.

As you watch the paper burning visualise reaching those goals and being totally successful in making the transformation that is required.

Say chant, along these lines:

Fiery transformation power of flame
May I reach my goals, life won't be the same

Allow the candles to burn out. Bury the ashes or throw them in the trash.

Tarot spell to get things going

Tarot cards can be used very successfully as focal points in spell work (and meditation). If you want to set something in motion or give a person or project a kick start or push it faster, this is a good spell to work with. I keep a tarot deck just for spell work, then it doesn't matter if the cards get wax or essential oil on them.

You will need:

A red candle
Lighter or matches
Ace of Wands tarot card
The Chariot tarot card
Eight of Wands tarot card

Light your candle and set it in a safe holder.

Lay the Ace of Wands card in front of the candle, to the left.

This card represents the forces to set in motion.

Now place the Chariot tarot card centrally in front of the candle.

This card represents control and the force of movement.

Take the Eight of Wands tarot card and place it to the right of the candle.

This card represents moving towards your goal and the end result.

Look at the Ace of Wands and visualise the beginning of your project or situation.

Then look at the Chariot card and see it all starting to move and action happening. Use the images on the card and really see the horses and the chariot speeding along.

Now to the Eight of Wands, visualise everything happening fast and the success of your goal.

Take your time with this and really utilise your visualisation skills.

Allow the candle to burn out.

Cleanse your tarot cards and return them to the pack.

A va va voom passion spell

If your love life needs a bit of a boost then this is a good spell to help bring back the passion.

You will need:

A red candle
An altar candle (any colour)
Lighter or matches
Essential oil such as cinnamon, dragon's blood or rosemary

Light your altar candle and sit quietly watching the flame. Visualise your love life filling with passion and a strong connection between you and your partner.

Dress the red candle with the essential oil, bringing the oil from the top to the middle and from the bottom to the middle – to bring passion towards you.

Place the candle in a safe holder. Light the red candle from the flame of the altar candle and place it in front of you.

Hold your hands to either side of the flame from the red candle (be careful not to touch the flame or burn your hands).

Feel the warmth of the flame and allow that energy to flow through the palms of your hands, up your arms and into your body.

Say a chant, something like:

Fiery passion and energy of red
Fill my body with flames to take to bed

Focus on the flame and sit with the candle until it burns out. You might want to have an early night...

Courage spell

We all need a boost of courage every now and then, particularly if we are about to take on something new to us or a situation we are unsure of.

You will need:

A red candle
Lighter or matches
Essential oil or incense burner
Incense or oil that you associate with courage such as carnation or fennel.
Black pepper corns

Start the incense or oil burner going.

Allow the scent to fill the air before you light the red candle.

Take a pinch of black peppercorns and drop them into the

incense or oil.

Say:

Courage and confidence come to me
With the fiery power of pepper you see
Fill me with the courage I need
And confidence to help me succeed

Focus on the candle flame and see yourself full of courage and achieving success.

Allow the candle to burn out.

Clearing Spell

Sometimes life puts blockages in our pathway. These can be cleared using the power of fire.

You will need:

A white candle
Candle holder
Matches or a lighter
Clove essential oil

Dress your candle with the clove essential oil, dressing it by applying the oil from the centre of the candle to the outer top and from the centre outwards to the bottom edge.

Light the candle and sit quietly.

Visualise any blockages being burnt away, allowing you a free and clear pathway to move forward.

Allow the candle to burn out.

House Protection

This is a simple but effective spell to bring protection for your house. Whether you want to bring about protection for when you are home or if you need to leave the house unoccupied for a while.

You will need:

Your visualisation skills

Sit quietly in your home and visualise a very large dragon either sitting on the roof of your home or hovering just above it. See him open his wings out wide and fold them protectively around your house. Remember to thank him when you return home or send him your gratitude on a regular basis if he takes up residence.

Protection Spell Pouch

A useful spell pouch to keep in your bag or coat pocket to protect yourself. This also works well as a little charm bag to hang in your car for protection too.

You will need:

A pouch, the organza bags are good for this but you could make your own from a spare piece of fabric. Just a square of felt tied with string or ribbon would work. If you want to bring colour magic in you could use black.

A thorn

A nail

Safety pin

Black crystal such as obsidian

A blend of herbs that you associate with protection, it also helps if they are fire herbs too. My suggestions would be angelica, blackthorn, black pepper, cedar, celandine, cumin, dragon's blood, fennel, garlic, ginger, hawthorn, juniper, nettle, rosemary, rowan, tobacco, witch hazel, wormwood. You don't need to use all of these, just two or three from the list.

Take your bag and add the items one at a time, charging each one with the intent of protection. Hold them in your hand and see them being filled with protective energy.

For both the thorn and nail, see the sharp points as protecting you.

Hold the safety pin and visualise yourself feeling safe and secure.

With the crystal, charge it with protective energy.

Obviously, you don't need all of the herbs and spices on the list, I would suggest just two or three of them. Be guided by your intuition and what you have to hand. Take a good pinch of each one, charge it with protective energy and add it to the bag.

Once you are done carry the bag with you, or pop it in the car or hang it in your home.

Keep a check on it, if it feels it needs it you can re-charge the bag as a whole or add a few new ingredients to it. Give it a shake to keep the energy moving.

Breaking bad habits spell

We all have them, some of them you can live with, others not so much. This spell will help you get out of a destructive cycle and leave those bad habits behind.

You will need:

A Devil tarot card
A white candle
Lighter or matches
Frankincense essential oil
A slip of paper
Pen or pencil
Cauldron or fire proof container

Place the Devil tarot card in front of you.

Dress the candle with the essential oil, rub from the centre of the candle out to the top and from the centre outwards to the bottom. This shows that you want to release and let go of the energy.

Light the candle and place it in a safe holder in front of the tarot card.

Take the paper and write down the habit you want to release, turn the paper around half a turn and write you name over the top of it.

Hold the paper in your hand and focus on the Devil tarot card. See the details, the image, the colours on the card. Visualise the bad habit you want to release and let go of.

Take the paper and light it from the candle, drop it into the cauldron and allow it to burn.

As you watch the paper burning visualise replacing the bad habit with a good one. See it turned around, flipped from bad to good.

Allow the candle to burn out.

Garlic cleansing spells

Garlic is really good for clearing out negative energy. Folklore says it is excellent for keeping out vampires too, but I am not so sure, I think they have gotten wise to it.

There are many ways to use garlic to cleanse and purify. You don't always need to use the whole garlic clove; I just use the papery outer skin for magical workings. The cloves of garlic get used in cooking.

Take the garlic peelings and grind them up with sugar. Sprinkle onto hot charcoal and use the smoke to cleanse the house.

Use garlic peelings ground with sugar and sulfur powder. Use on hot charcoal to create a cleansing smoke.

Take a couple of garlic cloves complete with skins and crush them. Mix with coffee beans or coffee powder and mix together. Burn on hot charcoal and use the smoke to cleanse.

Take garlic skins and crush with frankincense resin, grind and use on hot charcoal. Cleanse with the smoke.

Keep a string of garlic bulbs hanging in the doorway to your home.

If someone needs a bit of a direct cleansing, pop a crushed garlic clove under their bed or chair. Once it has worked its magic burn it. (The garlic, not the bed or the person).

Hot Foot Powder

One of the most well-known foot track magic powders is Hot Foot Powder. The usual ingredients are hot chillies, sulphur, cayenne pepper, black pepper and any powder that is hot or irritating.

Hot Foot Powder is sprinkled on the ground where your intended victim will walk over it. Once that person has stepped into it that powder will be carried with them into their home or car, taking the magic into their lives. It can be used to drive away unwanted people, make enemies leave or basically make people you don't like get out of your life.

To make your own powder you can use:

Cayenne pepper
Graveyard dirt
Chilli powder
Black pepper
Sulphur

I also use Hot Foot Powder sprinkled around the boundaries of my home to keep out unwanted visitors and to protect my house. A basic mix can be made with just chilli powder, cayenne and black pepper.

Four Thieves Vinegar

Legend has it that during the Middle Ages a band of four thieves stole from the bodies of those who had died from the plague. They made a lot of money in the process, but never succumbed to the plague themselves. When they were eventually arrested, they made a deal to share the secret of their protection from the illness in exchange for their lives. Their secret was a vinegar blend that they made and covered themselves in to ward against the plague.

Four Thieves Vinegar can be used for protection against illness, personal protection, banishing and cursing your enemies. Most variations can be used topically and ingested, but always check the ingredients first because some that are for topical use contain herbs that may cause sickness or even be poisonous.

Recipes will vary but the base is... well... vinegar! You can use white vinegar, but cider or red wine vinegar works well. Add to your cider, red wine or white vinegar any or all of the following ingredients:

Garlic
Salt
Pepper – black or red
Basil
Sage
Lavender
Mint
Mustard seeds

Add your ingredients to the vinegar and put in a sealed bottle or jar; leave in a dark place for three or four weeks. You can then either leave all the herbs in the liquid or strain it into a new bottle.

This Four Thieves Vinegar can be taken internally – one teaspoon a day to protect against illness. You can also use it as a gargle for sore throats. Soak a cloth in the vinegar and inhale to clear your sinuses. Add a couple of tablespoons of Four Thieves Vinegar to your bath water for protection.

To banish an enemy, you would make up a bottle of Four

Thieves Vinegar and then bury it under the victim's doorstep or porch, or you could even throw it at their porch so that the bottle smashes on their threshold.

To use it as a jinx against someone, use something personal from them such as a strand of hair or a photograph and put that into a bottle containing Four Thieves Vinegar, add nails and pins (nine of each works well), add a spoonful of graveyard dirt, shake the bottle and then bury it on their property.

Undoing or reversing spells

There are a few questions that I get asked on a regular basis, one of them is: "I worked a spell and it has gone horribly wrong, how do I undo it." It does happen, I suspect it has occurred for most of us at one time or another. Spells do have a habit of working in unexpected ways. There are a few pointers to avoiding spell catastrophes, but this is given in the smug situation of hindsight...

- *Remnants* – If you kept the spell remnants you can simply burn them, this will cancel out the original spell perfectly. This only really works if you didn't use fire in the original spell casting. If you used fire initially, burning the remnants could actually increase the energy of the spell, and ya don't wanna be doing that. Please make sure that you only burn safe items, anything plastic should not be burnt.

- *Details* – If you have specific details written down from when you cast the spell you can work a new spell to cancel each step. Beside each step, each chant, each herb or ingredient used make a note of the opposite. If you used moon water in your original spell you could replace that with sun water or fire. If you used an earth element you would replace that with an air one. Any herbs you used will need to be replaced with an opposing herb. Any words you used will need to be re-written with a cancelling effect. You might also like to work your reversing spell in the opposite order to the original. Think 'opposites and reversing' for all of the steps and ingredients.

- *Cord cutting* – Cutting cords also works well if you have bound yourself to someone or something and then discover that the situation is now overwhelming and you want out. This can be easily done with visualisation – light a candle and ground and centre yourself. Then close your eyes and see yourself and the other person with all the cords attaching each of you together. There may be one main cord or there might be several. Now you need to visualise each cord cutting and breaking away so that you end up with no cords connecting you. Finish the visualisation by saying something such as *'I cut the cords that bind us, I release the strings that connect us, I set both of us free'*. You might also want to work some self-care after a cord cutting, remind yourself that you are surrounded by love and happiness. You could also follow the cord cutting spell in this book.

- *Stop the magic* – A simple 'stop the magic' spell could also be used. Light a black candle and 'see' the spell you worked. Then snuff out the black candle and snap it in half. As you do so visualise the original spell falling apart and breaking, dissipating into mist. You could accompany it with some words stating the spell you want to stop and cancel. Bury the broken candle or throw it in the trash.

- *Don't…* – Whatever you do please don't use mirror magic or any kind of reflecting spell, as you were the person that cast the spell, the magic will bounce right back and hit you squarely in the face. I am pretty sure that isn't what you want.

- *Protection* – And don't forget that protection magic has

an important place too, keep up your protective guard to minimise any stray backlash.

Don't work a spell if you are really angry or upset, wait until you have calmed down and thought it through properly. Don't work a spell if you are drunk or high, who knows what chaos you could cause.

Keep detailed descriptions of your spells, write down what you did, how you did it, when you did it and what you used – if you have all that information to hand it makes it easier to undo. Keep your spell remnants if the working has a possibility of going pear shaped, particularly in the case of intents such as bindings and love spells. If you have the remnants of the working it makes it easier to cancel out the original spell.

Exercise
I always believe it is useful to keep a record of any spell work. Details of what you used and how you work the spell. It can be helpful as a reference to know how well the spell worked or didn't. It is also essential if you need to reverse the spell.

Blood 'n stuff

Now this is a subject that you will either find absolutely fascinating or you will skip quickly past this section and either is totally OK, it is your pathway, your journey and therefore your choice about what you include or don't but here it is just in case. I have included this here because I see bodily fluids as corresponding in general with the element of fire. Particularly blood.

Your body is the vessel that carries the magic, the energy and the intent but it is also very unique and individual to you. So, if you want to add the personal touch to any working you can literally add a bit of yourself into it. Or a bit of someone else…

If you are working magic for someone else or that involves

someone else, for instance a healing poppet, you may want to add in something of theirs that will link the magical item to them, let's suggest an easy option of a piece of hair or a nail clipping. The energy from the person will be in that very personal item collected from them.

Hair is often used as it is fairly easy to obtain and perhaps less intrusive than some of the other items. It can also be used like string or twine and work as a binding. Nail clippings are another traditional personal item used in magic even if it may involve rooting around in the bathroom waste bin to find what you need. I don't personally think they are quite as powerful as hair, but they do work well.

Menstrual blood is an ancient magical fluid and although obviously only obtainable from women of a certain age it carries an immense amount of power. This bodily fluid brings power, protection, love, passion, sexuality, fertility and lunar magic. You can add menstrual blood to most magical workings to link in yourself or a particular person, it can also be used in love magic to bind someone to you (think very carefully about whether you really want to go down that route). Menstrual blood can also be used to anoint your magical and divination tools to give them a strong connection to you.

To bring fertility bury a terracotta pot containing menstrual blood at the foot of a fertile tree and request blessings of the fertility kind from the tree, ask nicely and remember to compliment the tree on how wonderful it looks.

Blood can be obtained by pricking your finger (or someone else's) but please make sure you use a sterilised pin. If you have received tattoos then you can ask the tattoo artist if you can have the tattoo needle. (You may have to pay for it). The needle can then be used in magic as it has your blood imbued into it. I use mine for carving symbols and sigils onto candles.

Saliva – good ole spit. There is a reason why spitting is so rude other than it is quite a revolting habit, but saliva is actually thought to be quite controlling. It also brings the magical properties of protection and the ability to dispel negative spirits. Spit in the direction of a perceived threat to dispel negative energy, if you don't know what direction it is coming from spit over your left shoulder. On the positive side spit is also considered lucky and can transmit your will and intent, spit on betting tickets or lottery cards to bring good fortune.

Sexual fluids from both males and females can also be used in much the same way as menstrual blood although they have a more vulnerable magic to them. Female fluids have very strong fertility and life power magic and male fluid is believed to have very good healing properties.

Sweat, although I am not sure how easy it is to collect droplets. You can wipe a cloth across a sweaty brow or armpit and this can be used in sex and love magic quite successfully although it does have a more masculine energy.

Urine is, historically, one of the most common ingredients found in witch bottles that were buried in walls and chimneys of old houses. Funnily enough originally used to protect against witches. Your pee is obviously very personal to you and can be used in protection, territory and domination magic

Electronics

In today's modern world we encounter electronic gizmos and gadgets on a daily basis. Most of us use computers in some form whether it is a laptop, tablet or mobile phone. In and around our house we have a huge array of appliances that we plug into the electric current such as hair dryers or food mixers. Electricity and phones all work with energy. I associated that energy with the element of fire. You can work magic with all of these appliances. We all know that computers seem to have a mind of their own. By connecting with the energy of your appliance you can at least sometimes help them to stay happy and efficient. Placing crystals close to electric appliances can also help the flow of electricity and help prevent them from malfunctioning.

I have also found that spells can be very effective when worked on mobile phones. Setting a photo of your goal or desire on your phone home screen can create positive manifesting magic for instance.

Vision boards can be created on your laptop or tablet and saved as a file or set as your home screen giving a daily reminder of your goals. Apps such as Pinterest can work very well as vision boards, pinning images of your goals and desires to help them manifest.

Mobile phones and tablets can also be used to stream meditations and meditation music of all kinds. You can also find apps for oracle and tarot cards via your mobile phones. We have used a mobile phone at our open rituals as a compass to set the directions. The applications for using technology are endless really.

Colour magic

I love to work with colour magic. It brings its own energy to spells and rituals. Bringing in a colour to represent an element can help not only boost your magic but help you to connect with that element.

Fire is often represented by the colour red or orange. Both of those work for me. However, go with what works for you. I have listed below my idea for fire colours.

Fire colours

- *Black* – protection, ward negativity, remove hexes, spirit contact, truth, remove discord or confusion and binding for spell work.
- *Orange* – the God, strength, healing, attracting things, vitality, adaptability, luck, encouragement, clearing the mind, justice, career goals, legal matters, selling, action,

ambition, general success.

- *Red* – fire elemental, strength, power, energy, health, vigour, enthusiasm, courage, passion, sexuality, vibrancy, survival, driving force.
- *White* – purity, protection, truth, meditation, peace, sincerity, justice and to ward doubt & fear.
- *Yellow* – air elemental, divination, clairvoyance, mental alertness, intellect, memory, prosperity, learning, changes, harmony, creativity, self-promotion.

Fire divination

Divination involving fire is fascinating, most of the variants involve working with a flame of some sort obviously. I have found that results from fire divination can vary, fire is a tricky beastie when it wants to be.

Pyromancy – divination by fire and/or smoke, also called fire scrying. You can use a bonfire, fire pit or fire place. Get the fire going nicely then sit quietly and watch the flames. Ask a question and then watch for any images or symbols within the flames or the smoke from the fire. You can add to the magic by throwing a pinch (or a handful if you are working with a large fire) of dried herbs or incense blend onto the fire.

You can work on a smaller scale by lighting a candle. Sit quietly and ask a question, watch for any symbols or signs in the flame. This also works with incense, watch the smoke for any signs and images. Add to the energy when using a candle by dressing it with a suitable essential oil, to help boost the psychic energy.

With flames, think about how they act and the symbolism. A sudden flare of flame might mean problems or issues, but it could also be that you just threw herbs onto the fire, so think sensibly. Check the colour of the flames too, obviously orange and yellow are natural for a fire but if you get a blue tinge it may be a sign of spirit presence. Bright strong flames often signal a positive outcome. Flames in a circular motion can mean good financial news.

If the flames suddenly die down it can mean that something isn't quite right, or that the issue is coming to an end. The height of flames can also signify periods of time, short flames may equate to hours or days and tall flames could mean weeks or months.

Dividing flames or plumes of smoke can show two options, two or more pathways or separation. Watch the direction of the smoke (provided there isn't any wind to control influence it), this could point to the qualities of the four elements.

Botanomancy – divination by burning plant or tree leaves and branches and herbs. Often vervain or briar was used along with sage leaves. The plants were burnt and the smoke and ashes read. The fire was also listened to for any crackling sounds. The questions were sometimes carved into the wood before it was thrown on the fire.

Capnomancy/Libanomancy – divination by reading the smoke as it rises from the fire, often sacrificial fires. Cedar branches and shavings were burnt usually on holy dates and the patterns of smoke from the fire were read. Smoke was also read from sacrificial fires.

Causimancy – divination by burning various objects in fire. An item (whatever it might be) is offered to the fire and then watched to see how it burns, or if it even catches alight. Slow burning or not lighting at all was considered a bad omen.

Daphnomancy/Empyromancy – divination by burning laurel leaves in a fire. If it crackles loudly that is a good sign. Also, if the flames were bright and it burns quickly it foretold good news. If it didn't crackle or just smouldered slowly then the outlook was a bleak one.

Osteomancy – divination using bones. This seems to cover throwing bones as you would a set of runes and reading how they fall or watching bones burning in the fire and reading the cracks.

Scapulimancy – reading the cracks in a mammal's shoulder blade bones that have been heated in a hot fire.

Sideromancy – divination by burning straw with an iron. Iron was heated and then straw thrown onto it, the shapes, smoke, flame and patterns were then interpreted.

Ceroscopy – a reader will light a candle, ask a question and then drip wax from it onto a bowl of cold water. The answer to the query can be read in the shapes and images of the wax.

Exercise
Work with some of the fire divination methods. See which one works best for you and what sort of results you get.

Astrology

For those of you that work with horoscopes, sun signs and moon signs. The twelve signs of the zodiac are split into the four elements. What we generally think of as our zodiac sign is the sun sign, we were born under. We usually take on a lot of the characteristics that the sign corresponds with although we will also be affected by the moon sign we were born under as well. And of course, if you are working magic you can take into account the sign that the sun or moon is in to help boost your magic, which is what I am looking at here...

The fire signs are:

Aries – 21st March to 19th April – the sign of cardinal fire.

Ruled by Mars: Impatient, competitive, fighting spirit, confident, bossy, attention, leader, adventurous, possible diva traits and inconsiderate.

Qualities: Impulsive, daring, setting things in motion, enthusiasm, inspiration, force of nature, passionate, courageous, unconventional, joyful, individual, intuitive, sense of purpose, extremes, quick reactions, action, leader, decisive, original, risk taker.

Symbol: The head of a ram, perhaps even a fountain or the eyebrows and nose of a human.

Leo – 23rd July to 22nd August – the sign of fixed fire.

Ruled by the Sun: Dramatic, showy, likes the spotlight, leadership, likes praise, big hearted, generous, helpful, protective, fun but can be vulnerable or self-centered.

Qualities: Vibrant, confident, determined, outgoing, loyal, happy, busy, responsible, entertaining, humour, opinionated, fun, confident, proud, charismatic, dignity, glamourous, loyal, demanding, helpful, generous, friendly.

Symbol: The lion's tail or perhaps the creativity of the sun.

Sagittarius – 22nd November to 21st December – the sign of mutable fire.

Ruled by Jupiter: Happy, energetic, confident, big personality, travel, free spirit, optimistic, ambitious, busy, upbeat, wisdom, truth but can be divided and a procrastinator.

Qualities: Independence, adventurous, spontaneous, free spirit, honest, intelligent, philosopher, restless, excitable, funny, learning, goals, travel, free thinking, open minded, optimistic, lucky, curious.

Symbol: The centaur's arrow.

Exercise
Create some magical workings using the energy of the fire zodiac signs. Try using them on the corresponding date. What were your results and experiences?

Fire Blessing

Fire can be destructive but with that comes cleansing and the opportunity to wipe the slate clean and start again. Fire also provides some basic comforts such as cooked food and heat.

Always be respectful with fire, it is a wily beastie that definitely has a mind of its own. Give thanks to fire by feeding it with gifts of dried herbs and twigs. Light a candle to send your gratitude to the power of the flame. Send thanks to the sun, it provides warmth, heat and light for us to not only survive but to flourish and grow.

Ultimately the sun is a very powerful force, be mindful of that energy and what it can do for you. Working with solar magic can be just as rewarding as working with the moon (but that's a whole other book...).

Suggested Reading

Books for sources and reference along with other suggested reading:

A Kitchen Witch's World of Magical Herbs and Plants (Rachel Patterson)
Witchcraft into the Wild (Rachel Patterson)
A Kitchen Witch's World of Magical Food (Rachel Patterson)
Kitchen Witchcraft: Crystal Magic (Rachel Patterson)
Pagan Portals Animal Magic (Rachel Patterson)
Pagan Portals Sun Magic (Rachel Patterson)
Pagan Portals Brighid (Morgan Daimler)
Pagan Portals Lugh (Morgan Daimler)
Pagan Portals Blacksmith Gods (Pete Jennings)
Britannica.com
Ancient History Encyclopedia
Theoi.com
The Witch's Athame by Jason Mankey
Pagan Portals Sacred Sex and Magick by Web PATH Center

You may also enjoy

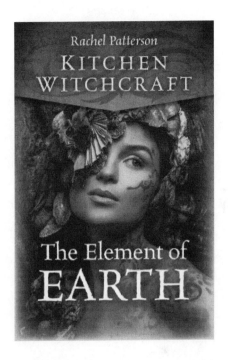

Kitchen Witchcraft: The Element of Earth
Rachel Patterson

The fourth in a series of books focusing on the elements.
Rituals, spells, correspondences, Elementals, meditations and practical
suggestions

978-1-78904-349-5 (Paperback)
978-1-78904-350-1 (ebook)

MOON
BOOKS

PAGANISM & SHAMANISM

What is Paganism? A religion, a spirituality, an alternative belief system, nature worship? You can find support for all these definitions (and many more) in dictionaries, encyclopaedias, and text books of religion, but subscribe to any one and the truth will evade you. Above all Paganism is a creative pursuit, an encounter with reality, an exploration of meaning and an expression of the soul. Druids, Heathens, Wiccans and others, all contribute their insights and literary riches to the Pagan tradition. Moon Books invites you to begin or to deepen your own encounter, right here, right now.

If you have enjoyed this book, why not tell other readers by posting a review on your preferred book site.

Recent bestsellers from Moon Books are:

Journey to the Dark Goddess
How to Return to Your Soul
Jane Meredith
Discover the powerful secrets of the Dark Goddess and
transform your depression, grief and pain into healing
and integration.
Paperback: 978-1-84694-677-6 ebook: 978-1-78099-223-5

Shamanic Reiki
Expanded Ways of Working with Universal Life Force Energy
Llyn Roberts, Robert Levy
Shamanism and Reiki are each powerful ways of healing; together,
their power multiplies. *Shamanic Reiki* introduces techniques to
help healers and Reiki practitioners tap ancient healing wisdom.
Paperback: 978-1-84694-037-8 ebook: 978-1-84694-650-9

Pagan Portals – The Awen Alone
Walking the Path of the Solitary Druid
Joanna van der Hoeven
An introductory guide for the solitary Druid, *The Awen Alone* will
accompany you as you explore, and seek out your own place
within the natural world.
Paperback: 978-1-78279-547-6 ebook: 978-1-78279-546-9

A Kitchen Witch's World of Magical Herbs & Plants
Rachel Patterson
A journey into the magical world of herbs and plants, filled with
magical uses, folklore, history and practical magic. By popular
writer, blogger and kitchen witch, Tansy Firedragon.
Paperback: 978-1-78279-621-3 ebook: 978-1-78279-620-6

Medicine for the Soul
The Complete Book of Shamanic Healing
Ross Heaven
All you will ever need to know about shamanic healing and how to
become your own shaman...
Paperback: 978-1-78099-419-2 ebook: 978-1-78099-420-8

Shaman Pathways – The Druid Shaman
Exploring the Celtic Otherworld
Danu Forest
A practical guide to Celtic shamanism with exercises and
techniques as well as traditional lore for exploring the Celtic
Otherworld.
Paperback: 978-1-78099-615-8 ebook: 978-1-78099-616-5

Traditional Witchcraft for the Woods and Forests
A Witch's Guide to the Woodland with Guided Meditations and
Pathworking
Mélusine Draco
A Witch's guide to walking alone in the woods, with guided
meditations and pathworking.
Paperback: 978-1-84694-803-9 ebook: 978-1-84694-804-6

Wild Earth, Wild Soul
A Manual for an Ecstatic Culture
Bill Pfeiffer
Imagine a nature-based culture so alive and so connected,
spreading like wildfire. This book is the first flame...
Paperback: 978-1-78099-187-0 ebook: 978-1-78099-188-7

Naming the Goddess
Trevor Greenfield
Naming the Goddess is written by over eighty adherents and
scholars of Goddess and Goddess Spirituality.
Paperback: 978-1-78279-476-9 ebook: 978-1-78279-475-2

Shapeshifting into Higher Consciousness
Heal and Transform Yourself and Our World with Ancient
Shamanic and Modern Methods
Llyn Roberts
Ancient and modern methods that you can use every day to
transform yourself and make a positive difference in the world.
Paperback: 978-1-84694-843-5 ebook: 978-1-84694-844-2

Readers of ebooks can buy or view any of these bestsellers by
clicking on the live link in the title. Most titles are published in
paperback and as an ebook. Paperbacks are available in traditional
bookshops. Both print and ebook formats are available online.

Find more titles and sign up to our readers' newsletter at
http://www.johnhuntpublishing.com/paganism
Follow us on Facebook at https://www.facebook.com/MoonBooks
and Twitter at https://twitter.com/MoonBooksJHP